1

Bottom-Line Organization Development

**IMPROVING
HUMAN
PERFORMANCE
SERIES**

Bottom-Line Organization Development: Implementing and Evaluating Strategic Change for Lasting Value

Merrill C. Anderson, Ph.D.

ELSEVIER
BUTTERWORTH
HEINEMANN

Butterworth-Heinemann is an imprint of Elsevier

Amsterdam   Boston   Heidelberg   London   New York   Oxford   Paris
San Diego   San Francisco   Singapore   Sydney   Tokyo

Butterworth–Heinemann is an imprint of Elsevier.

Copyright © 2003 by Elsevier. All rights reserved.

∞ Recognizing the importance of preserving what has been written, Elsevier prints its books on acid-free paper whenever possible.

Library of Congress Cataloging-in-Publication Data
Anderson, Merrill C.
  Bottom-line organization development : implementing and evaluating strategic change for lasting value / Merrill Anderson.
     p. cm.—(Improving human performance series)
Includes bibliographical references and index.
  ISBN 0-7506-7485-7 (alk. paper)
  1. Organizational change. 2. Rate of return. I. Title. II. Series.

British Library Cataloguing-in-Publication Data
A catalogue record for this book is available from the British Library.

The publisher offers special discounts on bulk orders of this book. For information, please contact:

Manager of Special Sales
Elsevier
200 Wheeler Road
Burlington, MA 01803
Tel: 781-313-4700
Fax: 781-313-4882

For information on all Butterworth–Heinemann publications available, contact our World Wide Web home page at: http://www.bh.com

10 9 8 7 6 5 4 3 2 1

Printed in the United States of America

Contents

v

CHAPTER 4

CHAPTER 5

CHAPTER 6

CHAPTER 7

S E C T I O N   T W O

Special Issues

CHAPTER 8

SECTION THREE

Case Studies

CHAPTER 13

*Knowledge Management: The ROI of Continuously
Leveraging Knowledge* 195

CHAPTER 14

*How Leaders and Change Practitioners Work Together to
Create Strategic Value* 207

Foreword

In the last decade, we have witnessed a significant and persistent trend of accountability in all major processes and functions in organizations. In the human resources consulting and organization development area, the trend is even more pronounced. Measurement and evaluation, value add, ROI, and impact are words that constantly reverberate in organizations today. In increasing numbers, senior executives and administrators are asking for the value—"Show me the money" is a typical expression. More precisely, "Show me the return on investment" is catching on by leaps and bounds. Articles, conference proceedings, and symposiums are laced with sessions discussing the need for techniques to demonstrate the value for organization development. From all indications, this trend will continue, requiring OD practitioners to show the value or face serious consequences.

OD practitioners are aware of the consequences. We can recall specific OD functions that have completely disbanded—many of them because executives could not see the value from this process. Yet, at the same time, we realize that OD, when practiced effectively, can add tremendous value. This book is an attempt to help OD practitioners show this value and highlight the results throughout the process.

The organization development field is ripe for this methodology. The need is stronger than ever before and the techniques and practice have been developed and refined.

The OD field often faces a dilemma with this issue. Within the human resources and human capital arena, no process is more appropriate for showing value than organization development. Most OD projects begin

ix

with an important business need that's often easy to measure. Yet many OD projects fail to show the value to those key stakeholders that want to know. Part of this dilemma is the reluctance of OD practitioners to be held accountable for their performance and show senior executives the payoff of their efforts. "Trust us, this is a great process that will add value" has been the theme for many practitioners. However, in most organizations, this won't sell in today's climate.

This book is unlike any other on the market. While there are great books on organization development and consulting, no book integrates the results-based approach in the kind of detail and precision that Merrill offers. The material is presented in a way that is basic, fundamental, understandable, and useable to OD practitioners. Credible, conservative, and valid techniques are highlighted. This book should be an indispensable tool for practitioners alongside other major works that have proven to be valuable in terms of OD methods and techniques.

The approach is simple: focus on value and ROI throughout the OD assignment. More specifically, Merrill shows how to approach the engagement with very clear business needs that translate specifically into application and impact objectives. He shows how to provide feedback to keep the focus on results and keep the project on track. He shows how the value can be determined early and often throughout the project, culminating with the impact analysis, and even ROI. Along the way, he shows how to tackle the sensitive and difficult issues of isolating the effects of the OD project from other influences and converting data to monetary value. The approach is straightforward, simple, and yet powerful to achieve what is needed in the OD field.

Merrill is the right person to write this book at this time. He is an outstanding OD consultant and has been Director of OD in several major organizations. With his tremendous expertise in this field, I regard him as one of the leading practitioners in OD. He's also an outstanding researcher, documenting his work in several publications, including a major contribution to OD, *Fast Cycle Organization Development: A Fieldbook for Organizational Transformation*. Merrill has used his consulting assignments to prove out the theories and practices involved in developing this manuscript. Focusing on accountability, he helps many clients tackle the challenging issue of measuring results. Merrill has a business focus on everything he challenges. He's always concentrating on the "so whats" and the value-add issues around any process or function. He brings his business focus to this book and to the processes in the book.

Tackling OD from the results-based focus and showing the impact of OD from the beginning to the end has three major payoffs. First, it will enhance the value of organization development in projects and assignments. Second, it will improve relationships with key stakeholders, particularly the clients and sponsors of these projects because they will see the value of the work. Third, it will develop excellent strategic marketing information to show prospective clients the value of OD projects. With these payoffs and the needs for this book, we are excited about making this contribution to the OD field. This is an excellent addition to our series on Improving Human Performance.

Jack J. Phillips, Ph.D.
The Jack Phillips Center for Research
a division of FranklinCovey

Preface

In 1997, when I was the vice president of organization development for a computer equipment manufacturing and services company, I invited Jack Phillips to teach our team how to evaluate our organization development (OD) programs. His message and methods caught on like wildfire, not only with our team, but with many people in the human resources function as well. Until then, I had thought that documenting a financial return on investment (ROI) for OD work was a great way to show business leaders the value that the OD project added and would hopefully encourage the leaders to sponsor additional OD consulting work. But Jack's message was more than this. The ROI methodology was also a way of *increasing* the value of the work that was provided. There is an ROI to ROI.

Incorporating evaluation methodology into the change management process is a powerful way to increase the value of the change initiative. The result is a new way of approaching organization development called *strategic change valuation*. This five-phase process shows organization leaders and change practitioners how to maximize the value from people and change initiatives. Ideally, readers will apply this valuation process in its entirety, but realistically, this will often not be the case. Chapters are presented to adapt the process to a variety of situations. As a business leader, have you ever received a "deer in the headlights" look when you asked your OD manager about the tangible value an initiative added to the business? The chapter on ROI "on the fly" is intended to help leaders and change practitioners evaluate the business impact of an initiative after it has been completed. As an OD manager, have you found yourself always left with the budgetary table scraps for funding—always coming after manufacturing, sales, and other business units have sated themselves? The chapter on forecasting ROI can help by estimating the monetary value that your OD initiatives will create for the business. This levels the playing field and puts investment decisions for OD in the same context as potential investments for manufacturing and sales.

Jack and his colleagues have experienced great success over the years in utilizing evaluation in the human resource development arena. This book extends this approach into areas of strategic, continuous change initiatives. Case studies are presented to illustrate how this has been done and how this approach benefits clients and change practitioners alike. I recognize too that many organization leaders and change practitioners will not immediately or warmly embrace this message. Many leaders are skeptical that people and change initiatives are capable of delivering the kind of tangible monetary benefits that investments in hard asset-based initiatives have proved to deliver. Rest assured, change initiatives can and do deliver the goods. The strategic change valuation process translates these benefits into tangible business benefits. Change practitioners are leery that an evaluation-based approach to change will somehow debase the art of their practice, but it doesn't. Integrating evaluation and change management opens new doors for capturing and increasing the value of change initiatives.

I wrote this book from the perspective of someone who has been there. I've been asked by senior leaders "what have you done for me lately?" and responded by documenting monetary benefits of initiatives I have managed. I have watched funding for strategic change initiatives wither on the vine while other hard asset initiatives seemed to be awash in investment money. This book points the way toward how we can level the playing field. The merit of change initiatives and hard asset initiatives will be judged according to the same rules. Bottom-line OD is no panacea. It does, however, represent a proven approach to capturing and delivering tangible monetary value to the organization. Following this approach sends the message that investing in people and strategic change initiatives is also investing in the business. Change initiatives are to be viewed not merely as a cost to be endured, but rather as a valuable contributor to the business.

I wrote this book with many people I have known and worked with in my life in mind. People such as the clients, initiative sponsors, and organization leaders with whom I have had the privilege of serving; the OD and learning consultants with whom I have worked; external and internal consultants who have carried the load in deploying strategic change initiatives; managers of business and support functions who have worked hard every day doing their "day job" as well as deploying change initiatives; and finally, the human resource professionals who receive little praise when things go right but get a world of hurt when things don't. To all I salute you: This book's for you!

Merrill Anderson
Johnston, Iowa
2003

Acknowledgments

I have been fortunate to have so many people contribute to my learning and professional growth. My wife, Dianna, who is an accomplished coach and consultant, has enriched my understanding of how to be more effective as a consultant and challenged me to be the best that I can be. Jack Phillips is a valued mentor and is always willing to share his extensive experiences and insights. Patti Phillips has demonstrated to me the highest qualities of consulting that combines thought leadership with practical know-how. Many clients have shaped my thinking about strategic change and accepted me as a partner to create value in their organizations. Some of these experiences are captured in this book. The editing and production teams at Butterworth–Heinemann/Elsevier Science have been outstanding and made the production process as painless as possible.

CHAPTER 1

Introduction to Bottom-Line OD

Business leaders today face a conundrum: making bold moves to increase their company's value when so much of this value is intangible. Human capital is the new arena for increasing shareholder value. Learning, knowledge management, and the inherent capability of an organization to renew itself and grow are the new sources of competitive advantage. Although these sources offer great promise, they are also elusive. In 1900, all but 5% of a company's value was locked up in hard, tangible assets. Today, this percentage is less than half (45%). The remaining value of a company consists of intangible assets such as learning, knowledge, leadership, and the full talents of all employees—in short, human capital.

Human capital represents a potent source of competitive advantage. How can business leaders leverage human capital and create competitive advantage when they have such a difficult time measuring the impact and outcomes of human capital initiatives? In other words, how can leaders manage what they cannot measure? Leaders so far have had limited success in trying to do so. Some people may be tempted to suggest that leaders should just resign themselves to an intangible world and accept defeat when it comes to managing human capital. This suggestion cuts leaders off from powerful sources of competitive advantage. It's too early to throw in the towel.

Bottom-line OD tackles this issue head-on and demonstrates how leaders and change practitioners can tame the intangibles. Section Three of this book contains case studies that demonstrate how seemingly intangible initiatives designed to increase human capital can be evaluated in tangible terms: how these initiatives created monetary value for the business. The evaluation process was also a discovery process. New ways were found to increase the value of these initiatives to the business. In becoming measurable, these strategic initiatives became manageable assets of the business and rich sources of competitive advantage.

Do these case studies capture all of the value of the strategic initiative? Clearly no. Is there still a considerable amount of untapped and intangible value? Clearly yes. This does not mean, however, that the evaluation effort failed—quite the opposite in fact. Combining intangible value with monetary value enriches our understanding of how the strategic initiative created value and expands the horizons for subsequent actions. Business leaders have a more complete picture about how to leverage human capital for competitive advantage. By knowing what works, leaders can take specific actions that increase the value of human capital for the organization.

FLAVOR-OF-THE-MONTH APPROACHES TO CHANGE

Value is the name of the game. Strategic change initiatives are intended to unlock the value of human capital and create value for the business. Unfortunately, business leaders have often been disappointed with the outcomes of the strategic change initiatives they have deployed. Some have been successful while most strategic change initiatives have not lived up to expectations. The response of many business leaders was to immediately launch another strategic change initiative in the hope that the latest initiative would somehow be successful. Soon, the organization was hosting a parade of change initiatives. These became known as the "flavor of the month" or "change *du jour*" programs and were soon regarded by employees with pessimism. This pessimism was fueled by people's perceptions that this parade of initiatives had little bearing on improving business results. Leaders also began to lose patience—and faith—that these initiatives were going to bear fruit. The ability to clearly demonstrate tangible, significant results can be the difference between the initiative that dies on the vine and the initiative that flourishes.

BOTTOM-LINE OD: BREAKING THE MOLD

This brings us to the crux of the challenge: demonstrating bottom-line value from people and change initiatives. For many strategic change initiatives, the missing piece has been a formal evaluation process that identifies the monetary as well as the intangible value of the initiative.

This evaluation process also clarifies the unique contribution that the initiative made to achieve the top goals of the organization. Bottom-line OD takes this challenge head-on. A new process is introduced—the strategic change valuation process—that merges evaluation methodology with change management practices. Leaders and change practitioners have a new way of thinking about maximizing the value from people and change initiatives. Bottom-line OD also presents some practical tools and proven methodologies for measuring—and increasing—the value from strategic change initiatives:

☐ *Formally link top business goals to change initiative objectives.* It is not enough to tacitly assume that change initiatives will affect the top business goals. A vague connection of the initiative to the business goals will later lead to a vague understanding about how the initiative added value to the business. Specific, measurable outcomes of the change initiative are identified and linked to one or more business goals. A clear line-of-sight linkage is drawn from the initiative to the goals so that it is clear what value the initiative is adding to the business.

☐ *Develop evaluation objectives that guide change management activities.* Evaluation objectives are developed for each initiative objective. This makes it clear how the success of the initiative will be measured. Expectations of business leaders for the initiative can be based on the evaluation objectives. Change practitioners can be held accountable to deliver the benefits as defined by these evaluation objectives. The change management process becomes more focused and effective because change activities are geared to achieving specific measurable objectives.

☐ *Maximize the success of initiative deployment.* Evaluation is a dynamic process. There are many points along the road of deployment—signposts, if you will—that indicate how well the deployment is proceeding. If one signpost indicates that people are not effectively following the new work process, then actions must be taken immediately to correct the situation. In this way, evaluation increases the value from the initiative. Corrective action steps nip the issue in the bud before it blossoms into a full-blown problem.

☐ *Isolate the effects of the initiative to produce business results.* The strategic change initiative is one of possibly many influences on business goal performance. Understanding the impact of the initiative on the business requires the effects of the initiative to be isolated from all other potential factors. Proven evaluation methodology is employed to isolate the effects of the initiative, and in so doing, learn how the initiative added value to the business. The learning process yields many insights into how to better leverage the value of the initiative.

☐ *Convert the business results into monetary value.* Once the effects of the initiative to generate benefits have been isolated, the benefits are converted to monetary value. The evaluation objectives serve as the guide: Were these objectives achieved and how much monetary value was produced? The answers to these questions have a direct bearing on the business goals. The greater the monetary benefits of the initiative, the closer the business becomes to achieving its top goals.

☐ *Calculate the return on investment.* The total monetary benefits are known; however, what investment was required to produce these benefits? If the investment outweighs the return, then it's likely that the initiative was not a good bet for the business. The total initiative costs are tallied and entered into the ROI equation. The ROI is calculated and the results interpreted. In general, the higher the ROI, the better the initiative was for the business. Keep in mind, however, that the ROI is just one aspect of understanding the value of an initiative. Combining the ROI with the intangible benefits produced by the initiative completes the picture of how the initiative added value.

☐ *Leverage evaluation to sustain strategic change.* Having a complete picture of how the initiative added value opens up new levels of understanding and new avenues for sustaining the gains. When deployment of the initiative has concluded, it is important to reflect on what happened well and what can be improved. Recommendations are made that sustain the gains made during deployments and offer new ideas for increasing the future value of the initiative. New strategic change initiatives may be suggested. The business builds on its successes to get ever closer to achieving its strategy and goals.

How This Book Is Organized

This book is organized into three sections and concludes with a chapter that integrates and deepens the learning from bottom-line OD. The first section explains the process of strategic change valuation. This process is at the heart of bottom-line OD because it explains how evaluation and change management are integrated to produce a powerful approach to strategic change. Next, in the second section, special issues are addressed that will enhance utilization of the strategic change valuation process. The third section presents case studies that show how this process has been applied to the latest, state-of-the-art change initiatives.

Section One: Strategic Change Valuation

Bottom-line OD fully integrates evaluation methodology into a strategic change management process. This new approach to change—strategic change valuation—is presented in five phases. These phases—diagnosis, design, development, deployment, and reflection—are central to change management, and each prominently features evaluation methodology. Key process steps are illustrated with case study examples to show in practical terms how bottom-line OD is done. Readers will learn how the combination of evaluation and change management represents a powerful force for creating successful and sustainable strategic change. Chapter 2 explains the strategic change valuation process, and then a chapter is devoted to each of the five phases of the process.

CHAPTER 2: THE FIVE PHASES OF STRATEGIC CHANGE VALUATION

This chapter provides an overview of the entire strategic change valuation process. The linkage and interdependencies of these five phases become clear.

CHAPTER 3: DIAGNOSE PERFORMANCE GAPS TO ACHIEVE BUSINESS GOALS

The process begins with understanding the needs of the business. A diagnosis is undertaken to flesh out the gap between the current performance of the organization and the performance that is required in the future to achieve business goals. An initiative is proposed to close the performance gap. The business case spells out how the initiative will improve the business, estimate the costs for doing so, and make recommendations for moving forward.

CHAPTER 4: DESIGN THE SOLUTION TO ACHIEVE STRATEGIC CHANGE OBJECTIVES

Once the business case is approved, the next step is to organize a change coalition. This coalition consists of the initiative sponsor, the change practitioner, and many key stakeholders and constituents. Rapid proto-typing is used to accelerate the design of the initiative. A statement of work is produced that provides a description of the initiative, as well as its objectives, timing, and deliverables.

Chapter 5: Develop a Change Plan with Evaluation Objectives

A comprehensive change management plan is developed to carry out the statement of work. Evaluation objectives are developed based on the initiative objectives. Change activities are planned that will ulti-mately lead to achieving the evaluation objectives. Because evaluation objectives are linked via the initiative objectives to the business goals, completing the change activities are directly seen as important steps to achieve the goals. This is the time to think about how best to isolate the effects of the initiative on achieving the goals. The change plan offers many options to set up comparison groups and define pre- and post-evaluation opportunities that will contribute to isolating the effects.

Chapter 6: Deploy the Strategic Change Initiative and Evaluate Progress

Deployment is where the rubber meets the road. Pilots may be conducted to work out any deployment issues and ensure that full-scale deployment will be successful. Pilots also offer an opportunity to forecast the ROI based on real data. Signposts are established during deployment to indi-cate what is and is not working, and to point to corrective action steps.

Chapter 7: Reflect on the Business Impact Utilizing Post-Initiative Evaluations

When the initiative has been fully deployed, all of the final data are col-lected. Hard data are separated from soft data. Then, the hard data are converted to monetary benefits. Only those benefits that are directly a result of the initiative are included in further analysis. Total initiative costs are tabulated, and the return on investment is calculated. A com-plete story is assembled about how the initiative created value for the business. Recommendations are made to further leverage the initiative and benefits in the future.

Section Two: Special Issues

This section examines three issues of particular importance for bottom-line OD: forecasting ROI, using surveys to collect ROI data, and evaluating an initiative only after the initiative has been deployed.

CHAPTER 8: FORECASTING ROI

This chapter illustrates how to forecast the ROI of strategic change initiatives, much like the forecasting is done for other potential business investments. Forecasting not only improves decision making about the change initiative, but it also installs a discipline in how the initiative is designed and deployed. This discipline increases accountability for results and ultimately ensures that the results will be delivered.

CHAPTER 9: TRICKS OF THE TRADE: USING SURVEYS TO COLLECT ROI DATA

Virtually all evaluation efforts rely in part on data from surveys. Consequently, it is important for change practitioners to learn how best to construct questionnaires and utilize surveys for conducting the ROI analysis. This chapter presents the tricks of the trade and practical know-how in order to best use surveys.

CHAPTER 10: ROI ON THE FLY: EVALUATING AN INITIATIVE AFTER IT HAS BEEN DEPLOYED

The real power of evaluation comes by building evaluation into the change management process; however, it is more common that the evaluation is conducted well after the initiative has been deployed. When the CEO asks: "What did this initiative do for the business?" launching an evaluation effort is the likely response. This chapter adapts bottom-line OD methodology to evaluate a program after it has been deployed. Readers will learn the quickest and most effective way possible to answer this CEO's question.

Section Three: Case Studies

Brief case studies are utilized throughout the first two sections of the book to illustrate specific aspects of strategic change valuation. The third section of the book presents complete case studies that take readers through the entire process of applying bottom-line OD to three types of strategic change initiatives: executive coaching, organization capability, and knowledge management. Readers will gain a holistic perspective of how to make the seemingly intangible benefits of these initiatives tangible. In all three cases, the benefits of these initiatives are isolated, these benefits are converted to monetary value, and ROI is calculated.

Chapter 11: Executive Coaching: The ROI of Building Leadership One Executive at a Time

Executive coaching has emerged as a major initiative to offer highly personalized development and to build leadership capability. How effective is coaching in delivering bottom-line benefits to the business? This case study shows how a telecommunications company earned an ROI over 700% through coaching 43 of its aspiring leaders.

Chapter 12: Organization Capability: The ROI of Aligning an Organization to Strategy

Having a strategy is one thing, but implementing it is another. This case study discusses how an inventory and distribution unit of a computer manufacturer set out on a bold new course. Very quickly it was obvious to the leadership team that their organization was not capable of implementing the new strategy. They quickly assessed what the main capability gaps were and closed these gaps. As a result, the organization was better aligned to the strategy, and they gained a 1000% ROI in the bargain.

Chapter 13: Knowledge Management: The ROI of Continuously Leveraging Knowledge

This case study details a large equipment manufacturer that implemented an Internet-based knowledge management system, which enabled people from all over the world to connect and share. Communities of practice sprang up that organized people with like needs and interests. These communities became a place to ask questions, solve problems, and make decisions. The ROI study showed that these communities also contributed bottom-line value to the business. Overall, it was estimated that the knowledge management system generated an ROI of more than 600%.

The final chapter, Chapter 14, How Leaders and Change Practitioners Work Together to Create Strategic Value, integrates the theory, the case studies, and the learning to better prepare readers to implement bottom-line OD in their respective organizations.

MAXIMIZING VALUE WITH BOTTOM-LINE OD

Bottom-line OD presents a powerful approach to maximizing the value from strategic change initiatives. Evaluation methodology offers a structured approach to gain insights into both the process and the outcomes of implementing strategic initiatives. By weaving measurement into the fabric of strategic change, evaluation becomes more than just a measuring stick—it becomes a structured approach to increase the business value of the strategic change initiative. This approach creates a platform for conversations about how the change is achieving its objectives and how the initiative may best be leveraged to benefit the business. Business leaders become better positioned to manage change as a business activity.

SECTION ONE

Strategic Change Valuation

This section presents the processes and tools for executing bottom-line OD. Change management and evaluation methodologies are melded together to create the strategic change valuation process. This five-phase process begins with diagnosing performance gaps in an organization that thwart achieving business goals. A business case is developed that shows how remedying these performance gaps will produce value for the business and at what cost. The next phase deals with designing the solution to achieve specific strategic change objectives. Rapid prototyping quickly yields a workable solution that the client approves. A statement of work presents the activities, timing, and deliverables of the strategic change initiative that defines the development and deployment of the initiative. The third phase is to develop a change plan with specific measurable evaluation objectives. Plans are made to utilize pilots and the course of deployment to isolate the effects of the initiative. The fourth phase involves deploying the strategic change initiative and evaluating progress throughout deployment. Midcourse corrections are taken that increase the overall value of the initiative. The fifth and final phase deals with reflecting on the business impact of the initiative utilizing post-initiative evaluations. Hard data are culled from soft data, benefits are converted to monetary value, and the direct contribution of the initiative to produce these benefits is isolated from other potential influences. Total initiative costs are tallied and ROI is calculated. This section closes with a discussion about how best to leverage the insights created by the strategic change valuation process.

CHAPTER 2

The Five Phases of Strategic Change Valuation

Strategic change initiatives often fail because they were not grounded in the business: change objectives were not clearly linked to key business goals; evaluation of the change, if done at all, was not focused on the key drivers of change; and feedback about the progress of implementation was too sparse to support making midcourse corrections and improve deployment. Bottom-line OD changes this situation. Integrating evaluation into change management raises the bar on making strategic change happen: A clear line-of-sight is drawn from the key business goal to the initiative objectives; effective evaluation is built around the initiative objectives; and signposts are set up to provide leaders and change practitioners with timely intelligence on which to make meaningful midcourse corrections during deployment.

The strategic change valuation process is at the heart of bottom-line OD. This five-phase process follows widely accepted change management principles and practices, but with an added kicker: evaluation. With bottom-line OD, evaluation is not some bolt-on accessory or to be placed behind a glass door and used only during emergencies. Evaluation is as much a part of the change process as any other aspect of change management: sponsorship, engagement, or communications. These other aspects of change management are improved when evaluation is added into the mix. Sponsorship grows stronger as tangible monetary benefits of the initiative become apparent. Employees become much more engaged in the change process because they see the tangible fruits of the labors. Communication messages have more impact when these messages herald the realization of a substantial return on investment.

The five phases of strategic change valuation are as follows: diagnosis, design, development, deployment, and reflection (see Figure 2.1). The first four phases follow a fairly standard approach to change management. The fifth phase, reflection, is often neglected or relegated to a communications checklist. This is unfortunate because no true learning occurs without reflection. People do not learn by doing. People learn by reflecting on what they have done. The evaluation activities inherent within the strategic change valuation process generate a wealth of information that would not ordinarily be available. Organization leaders, change practitioners, employees, and others may tap into this wealth of information to deepen their learning about the change. These learnings translate into making substantial improvements in the functioning of the organization. In a way, this represents another important facet of the ROI of ROI. Reflecting on the deployment of change sheds light on how to be more effective at making change in the future.

PHASE 1: DIAGNOSIS

Diagnose Performance Gaps to Achieve Business Goals

The diagnosis sets in motion the rest of the change management activities. Misdiagnosis of strategic performance issues can be calamitous: Resources are poorly utilized, precious time is squandered, and key organization goals are left unmet. Bottom-line OD infuses a discipline in the diagnostic process that, without bottom-line OD, is often lacking. Describing potential performance issues in terms of tangible monetary impact on the business provides a down-to-earth litmus test of the diagnosis. This separates the wheat (cause) from the chaff (symptom). This also tempers business leaders who presume the answer and want to drive too quickly to begin designing a change initiative of their choosing. In this situation, leaders put undue pressure on the change practitioner to "get with the program" and forgo additional diagnostics. Continuing to dig deeper into understanding performance issues may be viewed by these particular leaders as delaying tactics. Chapter 3 begins with such a story.

There is a flip side to this approach as well. Expressing human performance issues in tangible monetary terms also tempers change practitioners who would like to simply "take the order" from the business leader. A comprehensive diagnosis is the immediate casualty. The risk of a misdiagnosis and its calamitous consequences are in the offing. Short-changing the diagnosis serves no one: Business leaders risk failing to

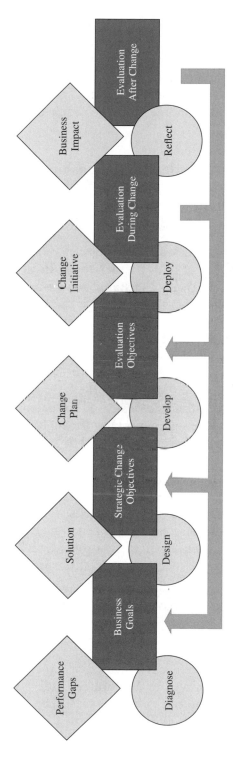

Figure 2.1 Strategic change valuation process.

make needed improvements in the organization; change practitioners risk designing and deploying initiatives with little organizational impact.

The chapter on diagnosis delves into three critical areas: the client (business leader)–consultant (change practitioner) relationship, linking performance gaps to achieve business results, and developing a winning business case. How this chapter addresses each of these three areas is briefly described as follows.

Building the Client–Consultant Relationship

The relationship between the business leader and the change practitioner will grow and develop throughout the course of executing the strategic change initiative. Bottom-line OD helps place this relationship on solid footing. This chapter discusses three types of relationships: customer–supplier, client–consultant, and partnerships. In a customer–supplier relationship, the supplier meets the stated requirements set forth by the customer. The customer issues the order, and the supplier takes the order and delivers the goods per specifications. There is very little in the way of collaboration to understand deeper performance issues, and as such, the customer–supplier relationship does not lend itself well to matters of strategic change.

The client–consultant relationship fits the bill for strategic change. In this relationship the consultant is dedicated to meeting the deeper needs of the client. This often requires working through the presenting symptoms. At the start of the diagnosis, the client may not know what the needs of the organization are. Often, clients respond to symptoms, and only through collaboration with the consultant will they come to understand the true needs of the organization. In a partnership, the client and the consultant come to share the same needs, not just understand each others' needs. This type of relationship tends to be the most enduring and satisfying of the three types of relationships. This chapter shows how evaluation activities can help these relationships to evolve and grow.

Linking Performance Improvement to Achieving Business Goals

The top goal (or goals) of the business is the starting point for diagnosing strategic performance issues. Inquiry soon focuses on better understanding the gap between current performance and the level of performance that is required in the future. Underlying causes for this performance gap are explored. These causes may be internal or external. Internal causes may be the adoption of a new strategy or setting new and higher business goals. External causes may be imposed on the organization by new actions of competitors or by regulatory changes. Understanding the cause, whatever it might be, guides planned actions to improve performance. Clear line-of-sight linkage is then drawn between the business goals and the objectives of the strategic change initiative. Evaluation methodology is employed to measure the monetary benefits of the change initiative in terms of helping to achieve the business goal. This section of the chapter concludes with the eight essential touchstones for conducting an insightful diagnosis.

Developing a Winning Business Case

The diagnosis culminates in the development of a business case. The business case summarizes all of the learnings from the diagnosis and sets the course for action. Bottom-line OD strengthens building the case for change by showing how the proposed initiative will contribute in a tangible and monetary way to achieving key business goals. The business case has five major elements: executive summary, strategic imperative, proposed initiative, business impact, and recommendations. The executive summary is nothing more than a distilled version of the other four sections. The other four sections consist of the following:

☐ *Strategic imperative.* The strategic imperative paints the big picture: what is the competitive landscape, what is required to win in the marketplace, how does the current organization measure up to these requirements, and what are the performance gaps. Performance issues are revealed and documented. Often, the consequences of inaction are enumerated.

☐ *Proposed initiative.* The proposed initiative, which will address the performance gaps, is described. The description of the initiative has enough detail so that readers can understand how this initiative will benefit the business. The full detail of the initiative is described in the next phase, the design phase.

☐ *Business impact.* Business impact outlines the investment that is required to fully design, develop, and deploy the initiative. Financial impact can also be articulated. In some cases, if the confidence in knowing the size of the financial impact is high, an ROI forecast can be completed (Chapter 8 covers forecasting in detail). Payback curves can be drawn that show how the return will, at some point, overtake the investment to produce positive cash flow.

Risk factors and assumptions are also identified so that readers have a sense of what must be managed in order for the change to be successful. An important contribution of bottom-line OD is to help manage the financial risk of the investment of strategic change. Mechanisms are put in place to make midcourse corrections, manage certain risk factors, and ultimately increase the monetary value produced by the initiative.

☐ *Recommendations.* Recommendations are made that point the way to best designing and deploying the initiative. These recommendations cover the gamut of effective change management practices, including sponsorship, governance, and communications.

PHASE 2: DESIGN

Design the Solution to Achieve Strategic Change Objectives

The diagnosis tells us what is wrong and why. The business case sheds the light on how to fix what is wrong. A solution must be designed to fix the problem. First, however, the leadership of the company must be organized and prepared to guide the change effort. The business leader, or client, works with the change practitioner to organize a change coalition. This coalition is made up of key players on the stage of strategic change: leaders, influential team members, and change practitioners. Governance mechanisms are established, and team charters outline roles and responsibilities for the change effort. Decision-making guidelines are communicated so that people know how critical decisions will be made and who will make them.

The design of the initiative is guided by a set of design criteria. These criteria are drawn from the diagnostic material contained in the business case. Design criteria state what the change initiative must have. Design options will be evaluated in terms of these criteria and a final design option selected. Objectives for the initiative are developed that have a direct bearing on achieving the business goals. The strategic change initiative is then designed that represents the best solution. These design activities culminate in a statement of work that summarizes the business need, describes the solution, outlines specific deliverables, and provides added detail on the investment required to move forward. The change coalition continues to play a vital role in developing this statement of work, approving its contents, and making the decision to proceed with developing the solution.

PHASE 3: DEVELOPMENT

Develop a Change Plan with Evaluation Objectives

The change plan is the road map for successful deployment. This plan shows how the initiative will be deployed and what it will accomplish. Bottom-line OD contributes to this plan in two major ways. First, bottom-line OD requires that evaluation objectives be developed. These objectives flow from the initiative objectives, which, in turn, flow from the key business goals. The evaluation objectives, then, serve as the key lynchpin between the business goals and the change plan that is dedicated to achieving these goals. These evaluation objectives are quantifiable and can be expressed in monetary terms. The evaluated impact on the business goals is tangible with implications for the bottom-line OD.

The second contribution of bottom-line OD is that a formal evaluation approach is developed in concert with the change plan. The two are inseparable, and for good reason. Deployment activities and timing can have a big impact on how well the initiative can be evaluated. Evaluation activities can improve the success of the deployment. The nexus for this dual interaction is, in a word, isolation. That is, how can deployment be done so that evaluation activities can pinpoint the contributions that the initiative made to the business goals and to isolate these contributions from other potential influences on these business goals?

Isolating the effects of the initiative is the Holy Grail of evaluation. Because evaluation activities are now part and parcel of the change plan, deployment can be designed to facilitate the isolation of effects. Key indicators are identified. Sources of data are tapped to show pre- and post-initiative changes in these key indicators. Pilots can be constructed to establish comparison groups to further isolate the effects of the initiative. Experts, end users, and other people can be called on to estimate the impact of the initiative to produce business impact. Few of these activities would be possible, or yield as high-quality data, if evaluation were left to be an afterthought to the deployment. As discussed in Chapter 6, integrating evaluation and change improves the quality of deployment.

PHASE 4: DEPLOYMENT

Deploy the Strategic Change Initiative and Evaluate Progress

Deployment is where the rubber meets the road. For many organizations, this has been a bumpy road. The actions described in bottom-line OD will smooth out this road considerably. Evaluation objectives keep everyone's eyes on the road; and progress on achieving these objectives functions like the dashboard in a car. People have real-time feedback on their progress. Bottom-line OD makes another contribution. Signposts are set up at certain points along the way that provide feedback on how successful the journey is being made. Signposts that indicate danger is ahead require immediate action. For example, a signpost showing that too few people are applying the tools and procedures outlined in the strategic change initiative will stimulate immediate corrective actions. If these actions are not taken, the full benefits of the initiative will likely not be enjoyed.

Value-Based Deployment

This chapter explores how value-based deployment opens up new possibilities for sustaining sponsorship of the initiative, engaging team members for effective deployment, and making midcourse corrections that ensure the success of the initiative. Strong, sustained sponsorship of the initiative is not a birthright. Change practitioners must work every day to ensure that sponsorship remains strong. A contributing factor to this is that the initiative is perceived as making solid progress on achieving the business goals. Perceptions are reality. Perceptions can be best managed with regular progress updates with the client and other key governance people. Communications can focus on key messages that reinforce the business value of the initiative. The governance team for the initiative can be leveraged in many ways to sustain strong sponsorship. This team can be tapped to overcome barriers to deployment, to demonstrate active sponsorship of the initiative, and to drive evaluation and communication activities.

Engaging people's hearts and minds in the initiative is essential for successful deployment. Deployment is hard work, and it can drain people's energy. Bottom-line OD opens options for renewing people's energy and keeping them engaged in the deployment. Meaningful performance feedback reinforces accountabilities and provides feedback on progress. People can be recognized for going above and beyond the call of duty. Deployment heroes are created. More broadly based communications can offer inspiring stories that keep people motivated to achieve.

Success, Thomas A. Edison once opined, is 10% inspiration and 90% perspiration. This certainly applies to deployment. The success of deployment comes mostly from the day-to-day blocking and tackling required to do all that deployment requires. Having the change plan is important, but the midcourse corrections ultimately determine success. These actions are based on the knowledge that evaluation activities generate. Signposts that trigger these corrective actions are established before deployment and are closely linked to project milestones. Deployment is a dynamic process whereby changes in the organization are made, the resulting impact is quickly evaluated, and corrective actions are taken.

Mastering the Mechanics of Evaluation

The dynamic nature of deployment requires, and challenges, the collection of timely and reliable data. Midcourse corrections based on old or unreliable data will likely make matters worse. The evaluation plan identifies the critical performance variables to be tracked. Data are collected for each variable. Timeframes are described for the base period and the treatment period. Performance improvements show up as increases made during the treatment period over the performance levels in the base period. Project cost data are also collected during the deployment so that, by the end of the deployment period, the total cost of the initiative is known.

Four levels of data are generally collected during deployment: (1) the reaction of the participants to the change process, (2) the knowledge and new behavior that people have learned, (3) how people have applied what they have learned to their work environment, and (4) how these actions have affected the business. The quality of these data are directly linked to the quality of the data collection processes and tools. All assessment tools and instruments are specifically developed to capture the required data and go through a series of pretests to ensure effectiveness. Assessment procedures and standards are established so that data are collected in a consistent and quality fashion. Data are analyzed with respect to understanding the progress of deployment in real time. Additional interviews or focus groups with people can be conducted to gain qualitative data and deepen the understanding of the organizational impact of the deployment.

Maximizing the Value of Pilots

Virtually every strategic change initiative features, or should feature, one or more pilots. A pilot enables certain aspects of the deployment to be completed on a smaller, more manageable scale. Implementation materials can be tested. Bugs can be worked out. Pilots can also test evaluation materials and processes and ensure that the effects of the initiative can be isolated. Pilots also offer the opportunity to collect solid data on which to base ROI forecasts.

Getting the most out of pilots goes a long way toward getting the most out of the full-scale deployment. There are six ways to maximize the value of pilots:

1. *Ensure that the pilot population reflects the greater organization.* The more representative the pilot population, the more the pilot data will have direct relevance to what might be experienced with the full deployment.

2. *Conduct usability testing.* This testing involves exposing a small number of people to certain aspects of the deployment process and materials. Ease of use and comprehension can be closely evaluated and changes to deployment processes and materials made to improve these materials for full deployment.

3. *Base ROI forecasts on pilot data.* This method for ensuring the value of pilots is also one of the most neglected. These forecasts indicate a range of benefits that can be realized if certain assumptions are met. Managing deployment to satisfy these assumptions will increase the likelihood of achieving the higher end of the range of ROI.

4. *Use pilots like a rehearsal.* Make sure all players knows their part and what is expected of them. Roles and responsibilities can be fine-tuned during the course of the pilot as balls are dropped or gaps in responsibilities become obvious.

5. *Use pilots to establish effective lines of communication.* Problems or unexpected barriers to effective deployment must be handled immediately. These issues cannot wait for the next monthly staff meeting to be convened. Pilots can show how rapid-response communications can be set up to deal with these issues during deployment.

6. *Conduct a debriefing immediately after the pilot has been completed.* All team members who were involved in the pilot can share their experiences and learn from the experiences of others. Best practices are aired and shared. People are better prepared to tackle the challenges of full deployment.

PHASE 5: REFLECTION

Reflect on the Business Impact Utilizing Post-Initiative Evaluations

With the deployment activities complete, it is now time to learn what impact the initiative had on the business goals and the organization and to reflect on how strategic change can be better deployed in the future. Data are analyzed to yield the essential information about the initiative and its organizational impact. There are five steps to accomplishing this analysis:

1. *Separating hard from soft data.* Hard data courses through the veins of bottom-line OD. Benefits that can be expressed in numbers represent the hard data of the analysis. This is not to say that soft data are not important because they are; however, the focus here is on showing tangible monetary value of strategic change initiatives, which requires hard data.

2. *Converting benefits to monetary value.* Units of measure, such as the "number of hours saved per week," are defined. There are four main categories for all units of measure: output, time, cost, and quality. Each evaluation objective will point to one or more units of measure. Standard values are used to convert these units of measure to monetary value. For example, a standard value may be that a manager's time is worth $75 per hour. Other standards may include a 40-hour workweek and 48 working weeks in a calendar year. These values would be applied against the output measure of "number of hours saved per week." A manager who saved 4 hours per week as a result of the change initiative would produce weekly benefits of $300 (4 × $75). Annualizing the benefits in this case is relatively straightforward. The $300 weekly savings is multiplied by 48 weeks to produce $14,400.

3. *Qualifying the benefits.* This step is a big one. This means that before the financial benefits can be included in the ROI analysis, it must be shown that these benefits are directly related to the change initiative and not to other factors. Fortunately, much consideration has already been given to isolating the effects of the initiative. For example, the deployment of the initiative—and quite likely one or more pilots—was designed to shed light on isolating the effects. There are three main ways to isolate the effects: pre- and post-initiative analysis, comparison groups, and expert esti-

mations. Error factors are also considered. So in the case of the manager producing $14,400 in annualized benefits, expert estimation could be used to determine both contribution factors and confidence factors. If end users (managers) of the initiative tools and processes estimated that using these tools and processes contributed to improving their productivity by 30% and that they are 70% confident in this estimate, then the qualified benefits of this one manager would be determined as follows:

$14,400 × 30% contribution (isolation) × 70% confidence (error) = $3024

The amount of $3024 of qualified annualized benefits would be added to the benefits tally. (Chapter 7 delves into this issue in great detail.)

4. *Tabulating the cost of the initiative.* Before the ROI can be calculated, the total costs of the change initiative are tabulated. These costs include participants' time, opportunity costs, consulting and vendor fees, materials preparation, travel, evaluation costs, and many other cost areas.

5. *Calculating the ROI.* These costs are combined to calculate the ROI and benefits cost ratio (BCR) as follows:

$$ROI = ((\text{benefits} - \text{cost}) \div \text{cost}) \times 100$$

$$BCR = \text{benefits} \div \text{cost}$$

It is important to note that the ROI is based on *net* benefits, whereas the BCR is not. Both of these calculations are useful in understanding the business value of a change initiative.

An example used in Chapter 7 used these calculations to gain greater understanding of a sales process improvement initiative. The total qualified benefits of this initiative were $134,400, whereas the cost to produce these benefits was $120,000. The ROI and BCR were calculated as follows:

$$ROI = (($134,400 - $120,000) \div $120,000) \times 100 = 12\%$$

$$BCR = $134,400 \div $120,000 = 1.1 : 1$$

At first blush it does not look like the initiative contributed much to the bottom line. According to the BCR, the initiative paid $1.10 for every dollar invested. In other words, the initiative paid for itself. The client, in this case the business leader, made the judgment if this return was good or bad. In this particular case, the initiative was done to support broader culture change objectives. The fact that the initiative paid for itself in the process was considered by the client to be icing on the cake. The intangible contribution the initiative made to achieve culture change was paramount.

The ROI analysis will have little effect on the client if it is perceived to lack credibility. The change practitioner and evaluator can take the following seven specific actions to build credibility for the ROI analysis:

1. *Emphasize the link of the evaluation to the top business goal.* The fate of the business goal, in part, rests with the fate of the initiative. The ROI analysis provides insights into new ways to achieve the business goal.

2. *Have the change practitioner identify and then work closely with the financial person who holds the greatest sway with the client and the governance team.* Having this financial person sing the praises of the evaluation is a guaranteed credibility builder.

3. *Gain credibility by being conservative at each step of the evaluation process.* Err on the low side on benefits and the high side on costs.

4. *Utilize the most reputable sources in the analysis.* A well regarded expert in the finance department can help identify reputable sources. ROI data are only as credible as the sources that provided the data.

5. *Use multiple measures when isolating the effects of the initiative.* Credibility grows with the results of each isolation method and as a consistent story emerges from several different sources.

6. *Circulate a discussion draft of the ROI report before issuing the final report.* This gives people a chance to contribute to the final report and increases their support and buy-in of the process. The more people see their fingerprints on the final report, the more they will support the findings and recommendations.

7. *Ensure the perceived independence of the evaluator.* If an external evaluator is not used, look internally at the finance or quality functions to provide evaluation oversight.

Leveraging Strategic Insights

Bottom-line OD evaluation activities have created a wealth of knowledge. It is critical to share this knowledge more broadly with the organization. People will develop a shared understanding of success, more readily buy in to the change process, and more directly align their efforts to achieving business goals. There are several ways to leverage knowledge in the organization. Key strategic messages can be developed based on the ROI results. These messages drive home the key lessons of change in the parlance of the receivers of these messages. Talk to employees in their language about the benefits of the change initiative. Build on these key messages to create and make available a common set of communication materials. Consistency is the key. Make it easy for people to deliver key messages with slide presentations, speeches, and talking points for more informal gatherings.

Leveraging insights from the ROI analysis can also be done by opening two-way communications with those who are inside as well as outside the company. Open the spigots of dialogue among employees, customers, suppliers, contractors, and other business partners. The value chain is strengthened as the merits and implications of the change initiative are shared and incorporated into everyone's activities.

CHAPTER 3

Diagnose Performance Gaps to Achieve Business Goals

Let's start with an all-too-familiar story. The new director of organization development was riding high. She had just come back from her first meeting with the CEO and, in her view, the meeting could not have gone better. The CEO asked her to act immediately on designing a performance management process. This new process would be deployed companywide. The CEO had just announced a set of aggresive business goals, and he believed that the performance management process would be an important pillar of support to achieve these goals.

In the days that followed this meeting with the CEO, the OD director organized her team and engaged several others in the new performance management design effort. This initiative got off the blocks quickly. There were many opinions about how performance management should be improved, and the OD director was literally working overtime to corral all of these opinions and stay focused on the design effort. It was her intention to design the initiative and present the design to the CEO as quickly as possible.

Sounds great, right? What more could a shareholder of the company ask for: a change initiative being designed quickly, strong support from the CEO, a responsive OD director, and a committed design team that has been quickly engaged in the effort. The answer turns out to be that the shareholder could ask for a lot more. Let's find out what.

For starters, the CEO has assumed that improving performance management will help the organization achieve its goals. How does he know this? What is this assumption based on? And if improving performance management will play a role in achieving the business goals, how big of a role will this be: 5%, 50%? The CEO is also implying that the current state of performance management is not sufficient for the company to achieve its business goals. He perceived a gap between the current reality of how performance management is practiced and where it needs to be in the future. But how big is this gap? The bigger the gap, the more effort it will likely take to close the gap and the larger the scope of the initiative will have to be. Enlarging the scope means committing more time and resources to the effort. How can the OD director launch the design effort without knowing the answers to these questions about the extent of the performance gap? Moreover, the fact that there are so many heated opinions about this topic suggests that people see the performance management issue differently. Consensus building at this point is critical to gain the buy-in necessary to develop and deploy the initiative later.

Now let's turn to the OD director. She is new in the organization and wants to quickly make a contribution to the company. There are many directions that her first meeting with the CEO could have taken. When he offered her the opportunity to embark on this significant initiative, she readily and gladly took the order. She reacted very quickly, assembled a team, and launched the design of the initiative. Herein lies the trouble: She reacted to the request, she did not respond to the real needs of the CEO or the organization. In fact, at this point, we do not know what these true needs are. In essence, the OD director and the CEO have skipped the entire diagnostic process.

How could this meeting have gone differently? For starters, the OD director needed to begin building a relationship with the CEO. She needed to better understand the issues he is facing, the priorities he is making for the organization, and the top business goals he is setting his sights on. Performance management, like any strategic change initiative, must be placed in this context. Performance management is a means to an end, not an end in itself. The OD director began designing an initiative without first understanding the business context of the initiative.

The CEO implied that there was a gap between the current state of performance management and what was needed in the future. The second way the meeting could have gone differently would have been for the OD director to begin exploring this gap. Then, at a deeper level, she could explore how closing this gap would help achieve one or more of the top business goals. Rather than taking the order, the OD director could have begun a dialogue with the CEO and explored these issues with him. Together, they could have drawn some critical linkages between business goals and performance management objectives. Then, they could make some informed judgment calls about the potential size and scope of the initiative and agreed on what more information was needed before the design could be undertaken.

The performance management initiative is likely to represent a major investment of time, money, and resources. This is an investment decision and should be treated no differently than any other business investment decision. Not performing due diligence on this initiative invites serious problems later. For example, chronic scope creep may set in, whereby the initiative gets pulled in several different directions at once and winds up trying to solve world hunger—not improve performance management. Without an explicit link to achieving business goals, the initiative has no center. Accountability for results is diffused.

The third way that this meeting could have gone differently was for the CEO and OD director to commit to developing a business case. This business case could have begun with articulating the business context for change, including the business goals and performance requirements. Next, the business case could have shown how improving performance management would have contributed to achieving the business goals. The objectives and major features of the performance management initiative could have been outlined. Potential monetary and intangible benefits could have been estimated, required investment stated, and if deemed appropriate, the ROI forecasted.

Committing to do the business case launches a very different series of actions. These actions will ultimately lead to a performance management initiative that produces greater bottom-line value to the business. Design without diagnosis is a prescription for disaster. This chapter explores in more detail three critical aspects of the diagnostics phase:

1. Building the client–consultant relationship
2. Linking performance improvement to achieving business goals
3. Developing a winning business case

BUILDING THE CLIENT– CONSULTANT RELATIONSHIP

In the preceding vignette, the OD director took the order from the CEO and ran with it. In so doing, she defined the course of their emerging relationship—that of a supplier delivering a performance management commodity to a customer. The trouble is, performance management is not a commodity, so the relationship was out of phase with the strategic nature of the initiative. The customer–supplier relationship is appropriate for most commodity transactions, but it is clearly not appropriate

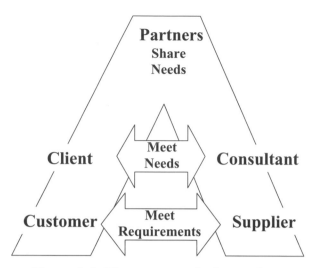

Figure 3.1 Three types of relationships.

for strategic change initiatives. These initiatives are highly complex and customized solutions to strategic business performance problems. If the customer–supplier relationship is not appropriate for strategic change, then what relationships are appropriate?

There are three basic types of relationships, which are illustrated in Figure 3.1. The first of these relationships, the customer–supplier relationship, is the one on which the OD director embarked. This relationship is characterized by the supplier meeting the stated requirements of the customer. Communications between the two are focused on ensuring that the supplier fully understands the stated requirements from the customer. There is little conversation about how the product or service being offered by the supplier can be adapted to meet the customer's underlying needs. This type of relationship is appropriate for many situations, but strategic change initiatives require more. This brings us to the next type of relationship.

The client–consultant relationship is characterized by the consultant digging deeper to discover the true needs of the organization. The initial request by the client is taken as a starting point, not an endpoint. The two people will have conversations that take them well beyond the performance issues they see on the surface and to the heart of the matter. For example, the OD director could have asked the CEO about the specific business impact he hoped performance management would have, or perhaps to explore the CEO's perspective on the performance gap.

These lines of inquiry are critical to placing the strategic change initiative in a results-oriented context. These conversations build links from the underlying business needs to the shape and scope of the initiative. As we will see in the next chapter, these links later form the backbone of the strategic change valuation process.

A partnership is a relationship based on meeting the shared needs of both partners. As the relationship matures between the client and the consultant, deeper value needs come to the surface and are shared. As partners, they experience a shift in not only working together to achieve the needs of the business, but also working together to achieve each other's personal needs. Conversations center around actions that simultaneously address the deep value needs of both partners. Trust grows. At some point in the future, the CEO and the OD director in our vignette may get to this point. This might look like the CEO and the OD director sharing their needs for increased recognition from the senior-level business unit leaders or perhaps satisfying their mutual need for increased family time.

The evolution of a relationship from a customer–supplier to a client–consultant to a partnership does not happen by accident. This evolutionary process is based on trust. As trust grows, so does the relationship. Trust may be defined as the firm reliance on the integrity or ability of a person to act in the future. The perception of integrity is largely based on how well people do what they say they will do. Trust is gained over time as people live up to their commitments. The greater these commitments, the greater the risk they face in meeting these commitments. Time and risk temper trust.

Building trust is also influenced by the potential benefits of the relationship. The greater the potential benefits, the greater the need for both parties to establish a trusting relationship to achieve these benefits. This trust dynamic can be expressed in the following way:

$$\text{Trust} = (\text{Benefits} \div \text{Risk}) \times \text{Time}$$

What are the implications of this formula for building strategic change relationships, and how does bottom-line OD contribute? First, with regard to the benefits, the implication is that the greater or more valuable the benefit, the more trust will grow. Bottom-line OD contributes to this by ensuring that the financial benefits and the business value of the initiative are explicitly made. All parties set their eyes on the prize. The entire bottom-line OD process is geared toward achieving these benefits and driving the value to the business.

The second implication is that lowering risk increases trust. Bottom-line OD provides business leaders and change practitioners with the added knowledge and tools to manage and minimize risk. The major risk factors for strategic change emerge during deployment. These factors include underutilizing resources and underachieving benefits. Bottom-line OD helps optimize resources by tracking and evaluating the progress of deployment. Critical and timely knowledge is gained about what is and is not working. Corrective actions can be taken. These actions ultimately increase the business value of the initiative, and in so doing, fully achieve the expected benefits.

Not all relationships are smooth sailing. Strong seas may rise. These storms must be detected early and properly navigated if the relationship is to stay on course and avoid the rocky shoals. Relationships typically go on the rocks not because problems arise, but because the problems are not effectively navigated and dealt with. In fact, successful recovery from these problems can even strengthen the relationship, just as the high winds of a storm can fill the sails of a ship that weathers the storm and makes it travel faster.

Two of the most common ways in which relationships derail involve clients who are guarded in terms of the information they share and consultants who do not adequately manage risk factors.

Relationships Derail When Problems Are Not Openly Shared

Clients often feel vulnerable with consultants around and may be initially reluctant to "air their dirty laundry" by openly sharing their problems. Consultants must be sensitive to these feelings and recognize the need for consultants to earn the right to work with the client and address critical performance needs. Consultants must rapidly become students of the client's business and demonstrate that they can work effectively with people in the client's organization. Understanding company culture and being sensitive to how things really get done in the company contributes to the consultant's effectiveness. Demonstrating these qualities to the client encourages the client to reciprocate and be more open with sharing needs and problems.

Relationships Derail When Risks Are Not Effectively Managed

Nobody likes surprises. This is especially true with business leaders and when the stakes are high. Strategic change initiatives require significant investment and carry high expectations for a return on the investment.

It is critical for the client and consultant to communicate frequently about the challenges and problems that inevitably arise during the strategic change process. If client–consultant communications are infrequent or ineffective, problems may grow and fester, and if left unattended, may put the entire change initiative at risk. Scheduling frequent communications based on evaluation data ensures that these problems will be detected early so that actions can be taken to fix these problems.

Linking Performance Improvement to Achieving Business Goals

Every journey must have a clear destination in mind. The destination for strategic change is discovered though the diagnostic process. Figure 3.2 illustrates what the diagnosis is expected to achieve. The starting point for any diagnosis is the business goal. This is the goal that the entire organization is dedicated to achieve. Introducing the new business goal also calls into question whether the current performance of the organization is strong enough to achieve the goal. It is important, then, for the diagnosis to take an honest look at where the organization is currently and where it must be in the future to be successful. The difference between current and future performance defines the performance gap.

Diagnostic efforts focus on understanding the performance gap, giving it shape and definition, and showing how closing this gap will help

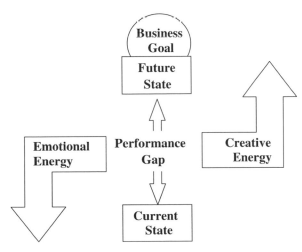

Figure 3.2 Describing the performance gap.

achieve organization goals. Defining this performance gap also creates tension. The greater the gap, the greater the tension. As tension builds, so does the sense of urgency to close the gap.

The organization is faced with two fundamental choices to close the gap: (1) change current reality to achieve the strategic vision or (2) scale back on the vision so that it more closely resembles the current reality. Realistically, in today's global business environment, scaling back on the vision is really tantamount to throwing in the towel and giving up the business to a competitor. It is not a viable option. This then becomes the challenge of strategic change: honestly describing the performance gap and changing current reality to achieve new levels of performance. Strategic change initiatives are launched to improve performance to the desired level and close the performance gap.

Committing to improve performance can be energizing for people in the organization. It allows them to come to grips with surfacing problems that they have likely experienced for years. The change initiative can offer people an outlet to apply their creative energy and solve the performance gap. Leaders must harness this creative energy and focus it on the strategic change initiative. Actions include engaging a diverse set of people on change teams, providing a platform for airing a wide variety of opinions and perspectives, and honoring those who tell it like it is without sugarcoating the truth. If these actions do not happen, the dark side of change will emerge. People feel discounted and ignored. Frustration sets in. Hope turns to cynicism. People's creative optimism turns into disruptive emotional energy. Not only does the performance gap not close, but it may even widen as people check out from their work.

CASE STUDY: DIAGNOSING DECLINING CUSTOMER SERVICE AT FOODCO

The CEO and chief procurement officer (CPO) at FoodCo (a fictitious name) asked an external OD consultant to determine why customer service was going in the tank. FoodCo buys and distributes a wide variety of food and food-related items for hundreds of grocery stores throughout the Eastern United States. More than 200 buyers' assistants work with their grocery store customers to ensure that the customers have the products they need when they need them. Timing is critical, given that many of the food items are perishable.

Customer service ratings had declined to 73% satisfied from 92% satisfied, as indicated by FoodCo's weekly surveys. The CPO believed that the recent merger with another company was largely to blame for the decline in customer service. The CEO, who was the architect of the merger, did not agree. Rather, the CEO believed that the recent restructuring of the procurement function into two distinct areas had confused the buyers' assistants and that they were not clear about their new responsibilities. The human resources director thought that all of this was hogwash. The buyers' assistants lacked a sense of urgency and did not feel a sense of personal ownership for customer service. What was needed, she thought, was a series of customer service workshops to "get their heads screwed on right."

The OD consultant began the diagnosis with an *ad hoc* team of people drawn from diverse backgrounds. This team included buyers, buyers' assistants, product managers, distribution managers, and human resources personnel. Data collection was extended to include grocery store customers.

Conversations that the OD consultant had with the CEO confirmed the CEO's growth goals for the company. He wanted the company to be the largest in the United States in three years. The key to achieving this goal was superior customer service. The current poor performance of customer service was limiting the company's ability to grow, and even worse, was lowering the entry barrier to competitors who would love to grab their larger grocery chain customers.

The diagnosis documented several examples of poor customer service: customers were passed from one company employee to the next to change existing orders; new customers had to contact several employees to establish an account; and buyers did not feel knowledgeable enough to talk with customers about new company promotions. Customers complained that they had to have a company organization chart just to place an order and that the process was too time consuming. Customers also resented having to learn about new product promotions and other company news in the trade journals, rather than from the company directly. Tensions were rising and it was time for action.

The OD consultant sat down with the CEO, CPO, and the HR director one afternoon to review the results of the diagnosis and explore some possibilities for action. Everyone was familiar with the findings from the diagnosis through participating in a series of update meetings convened by the OD consultant. The conversation revolved around the buying process. This process had been in place for several years, and the OD consultant questioned whether this process could reasonably handle the significantly higher volume of customers that the company currently enjoyed. The acquisition increased customers by 40%, and this sudden increase in the customer base stretched the process to its limits. The restructuring of the procurement area was theoretically a good idea, but theory and reality were at odds with one another. The restructuring created new roles and responsibilities that were out of phase with the way work actually got done in the current buying process. People were confused about which way to go—the old way or the new way—and frustration was growing. As soon as these process and responsibility issues were resolved, customer service workshops were clearly called for.

The diagnostic review meeting with the executives concluded with a consensus agreement that an initiative would be designed to reengineer the buying process. Then the structure of the organization would be adapted to make this process work as efficiently and effectively as possible. The OD consultant committed to develop a business case for change and forecast improvements in customer service. The CEO indicated that his priority was "to just move those (customer service) numbers up!" In his view the primary ROI was positioning the company for growth.

This case study illustrates a successful diagnosis. All parties mutually agreed to a clear path forward. The OD consultant did not directly challenge the different assumptions that each executive had made about the root cause problem. Rather, the consultant gathered a diversity of data and viewpoints that honored the perspective of each of these three executives. Each executive held a piece of the truth. The diagnosis pulled the pieces together to create a composite picture of what was truly happening. Honoring the perspectives of each executive also gained their buy-in to move forward with designing the solution.

What are the secrets to the success of diagnosing strategic performance issues? There are no secrets, but there are eight tried-and-true touchstones that characterize insightful diagnoses.

Eight Touchstones of Insightful Diagnosis

1. *Embrace diversity.* The diagnostic process is a journey of exploration into a complex set of issues and organization requirements. The more diverse the people who are invited to take this journey are, the more rich and comprehensive the information will be. A successful diagnosis requires fresh new ideas about performance issues and what can be done to improve performance. If you want out-of-the-box thinking, include people who are not in the box to begin with. Include in the diagnostic process people from a variety of business and functional backgrounds and from many levels in the organization. If appropriate, consider including customers,

suppliers, contractors, dealers, brokers, and others from outside the company to gain an even more comprehensive perspective. This is the approach the OD consultant took with FoodCo. Customers were interviewed and the data were included in the analysis. This action was critical, given that poor customer service was the issue.

2. *When in doubt, go with your gut instinct.* Intuition is often an underutilized asset. Human beings take in a tremendous amount of information every day, and somehow the brain assembles and organizes this information. The information is in our heads, but the real challenge is how to access the information. This is where intuition comes in. Intuition speaks to us with a soft voice that is often drowned out by the daily clatter and urgency to satisfy to-do lists. It is up to each of us to give intuition a chance and to tap into a wealth of information and wisdom. How do we do this? Well, when faced with a decision or selecting a course of action—do nothing. At least do nothing in a quiet space without any distractions for about 10 minutes. Allow your intuition to rise to the surface of your consciousness. Listen to your inner-voice. Understand the message and the meaning that is being presented to you. Then, as ridiculous or as unworkable as the message may sound—go ahead and do it anyway. Intuitive action reflects the deeper wisdom that each and every one of us has to offer. Have faith in your inner-voice.

3. *Be a student of the business.* An effective strategic change practitioner is also an avid student of the client's business. Being able to speak knowledgeably about the business is a quick credibility builder in the client's eyes. Read the last annual report. Study the balance sheet. Develop a list of questions and talk with someone in finance or accounting to get answers to the questions. Go online to the company's Web site. These sites typically contain press releases, articles written about the company, and other organization news. *Business Week* and *Fortune* magazines have archives with many articles that would relate to the client's industry and perhaps even have articles about the company. Many brokerages have Web sites that offer analysts' reports about hundreds of companies. The client company may be among these reports, as might one or more of the company's competitors. Gathering and reading this information firsthand enables the practitioner to develop unique perspectives and opinions about the company.

4. *Develop a point of view—don't be a business tourist.* Change practitioners have the wisdom, experience, and know-how to implement complex strategic change. As change practitioners gather information and learn about the company, they are in a unique position to combine their wisdom of change process with the specific content issues regarding the client company. This combination of process and content is the spark that can lead to exciting new ideas. It's okay for change practitioners to have opinions about what should be done—clients expect it. Develop a point of view, be willing to explain it to others, and be prepared to defend it if necessary.

   In the case with the OD consultant, he honed in quickly on the buying process as the primary source of the performance issues with customer service. He believed that conducting customer service workshops would have little impact when the process by which people delivered customer service was so broken. He presented the data that supported his point of view that customer service workshops should not be immediately conducted. When the HR director pushed back on this point, the OD director stuck to his guns and argued successfully that workshops would be the last thing, not the first thing, that would be done. The diagnosis pointed to other issues—process and responsibilities—that had to be addressed first.

5. *Show that you care.* Diagnosis is an analytical process. It is about numbers and data, correlations and statistics, financial indicators, and performance measures. Often, so much emphasis is placed on what we think about this analytical information that we lose touch with how we feel about what we are learning. It is important to show that we care and to share what we care most about. If, as a change practitioner, you feel that the course of action that a client is about to take is wrong, then make a counter-recommendation. But don't stop there. Speak with passion and commitment. Allow your emotions to give power and resonance to your ideas. Clients will more readily embrace your message when they believe that you care about them and their success.

6. *Inquire, don't indict.* Inquiry is characterized by seeking information by asking a series of questions. There are no value judgments, no right or wrong answers. Indictment, on the other hand, is making a value judgment. Indicting statements are those that attribute poor performance or some kind of performance problem to a person or a group of people. Individuals should never be the primary focus of a diagnostic effort. Rather, the emphasis should be placed on the processes by which all people work. Cite process

problems; don't blame people. These people are the ones who will have to be engaged to fix the problems. Indicting them will have the opposite effect. They will disengage and possibly become saboteurs of strategic change.

In the case of FoodCo, the OD director focused on the buying process and not the performance of the buyers' assistants. Although some buyers' assistants clearly had personal performance issues, this was not the focus of the diagnosis. In fact, the buyers' assistants welcomed the opportunity to fix the process problems, some of whom complained that these problems had been allowed to fester for years.

7. *Beware of sacred cows.* It is amazing what a diagnosis can uncover, and sometimes what is uncovered is too close for comfort for the client. A sacred cow can be an issue, a strategy, a perk or benefit, a pet project, or anything else that has special favor among the company's senior leaders. Occasionally, a diagnosis will conclude that a sacred cow is on the wrong side of the fence—that it is part of the problem and must be addressed. These issues, when surfaced, become hot buttons for leaders and as such don't bear close inspection. For example, leaders may emphasize the importance of increasing operating cash flow, but also insist that the corporate fleet of private aircraft be left alone. For the change practitioner, it is usually best to leave these issues alone unless there is a significant impact on performance. In any event, it is important for the change practitioner to know what the clients' sacred cow issues are so that these issues can be dealt with appropriately.

The OD director at FoodCo had two major sacred cows to deal with: the CEO felt that the contribution of the acquisition to the performance issue was off-limits and the CPO was in no mood to take the blame for his decision to restructure. The OD director wisely finessed these issues by discussing the impact of these two decisions in terms of the functioning of the buying process. For example, the acquisition increased customer transaction volume to such levels that the old buying process could not handle the volume. The buying process had to be reengineered to optimize the new organization structure. Had the OD consultant confronted the wisdom of these decisions directly, he probably would have experienced a quick case of *projecto interruptis*: The client would have stopped the project and sent the OD consultant packing.

8. *Open possibilities for the client.* The preceding touchstones have taken us through a process of understanding the client's business, gathering a diverse set of data, and developing a point of view about what must be done to improve performance. At this point, the change practitioner can open new possibilities for the client. Potential initiatives and courses of action can be offered to address the performance issue. The change practitioner does not jump to conclusions and immediately recommend a specific initiative. Rather, he or she has conversations with the client about several potential initiatives or options for an initiative. The benefits and concerns of each potential initiative can be reviewed and digested. These conversations result in a course of action that the change practitioner and the client mutually agree will yield the best results. This agreement opens the door to create a business case for formally recommending that an investment be made in the change initiative.

This is the point in the consulting process at which we concluded the case study with FoodCo. The OD consultant sat down with the three main decision makers to present the results of the diagnosis and offer possibilities for action. Their agreement to work on business process first, then organization structure, and then customer service workshops reflected the learning of each of the three client executives. They learned not only about how to improve customer service, but also about the process of strategic change. The next step for the OD consultant was to develop a business case that reflected these learnings and outline an initiative that would deliver results and prepare the company for growth.

DEVELOPING A WINNING BUSINESS CASE

The culmination of the diagnostic process is the development of a business case. The business case provides the rationale and the direction for strategic change. Specifically, it presents the performance gap, what can be done to close the gap, how the organization will benefit by closing the gap, and what investments must be made to make this happen. This represents a choice point for the leaders. Will they commit to closing the gap, or at least commit to design a solution that will close the gap? The business case can further propel the leaders and the organization into creative action.

The primary deliverable from an effective organization diagnosis is the business case. The business case presents the strategic and business context for strategic change. A clear, concise problem statement is articulated and linked to the business strategy. The proposed solution is described, along with the required investment. Measurement methodology is outlined with some sense of what the prize is for successfully fixing the problem. This business case provides the client and other decision makers with the information they need to approve going to the next step: a detailed design of the OD intervention.

The business case has five major sections: executive summary, strategic imperative, proposed initiative, business impact, and recommendations. The business case will also usually have an appendix of reference material that supports information contained in one or more of these sections. These sections may be sliced and diced in different ways to better match the needs of the client or the preferences of the consultant preparing the case. It is important that all of the following information is included somewhere in the business case.

The Executive Summary

The executive summary is nothing more than a distilled version of the entire document. Most executive summaries are about two pages. Given that most business case documents are more than 50 pages long, a considerable amount of distilling is required. Given the workload of today's executive, the executive summary is often all that executives will read. Therefore, the executive summary must deliver all of the critical information and messages that the executives need to know to make a decision about the initiative. This information includes:

- ☐ The purpose of the business case
- ☐ A crisp synopsis of the performance issue
- ☐ How resolving this issue will help achieve business goals
- ☐ The benefits of higher performance
- ☐ The investment required to achieve these benefits

A cover letter may be written that explains the decision areas and expectations for the executive when the business case is discussed in a leadership team meeting. If a cover letter is not used, this information can be included in the executive summary.

Strategic Imperative

It is important to make the connection from the business goals to the proposed initiative. This section begins with a summary of the company's competitive position and the challenges it faces. Business goals are presented, and the importance of achieving these goals is explained. Other business considerations are also discussed. These include areas external to the company such as regulatory issues, currency fluctuations, macroeconomic trends, and so forth, as well as areas internal to the company such as employee satisfaction, ongoing change initiatives, and other areas.

Next, the purpose of the performance diagnosis is presented. The performance gap is linked to one or more of the business goals. The point is emphasized that the business goal can only be achieved if the performance gap is closed. Data are presented to support this contention. This section of the report then describes what closing the performance gap looks like and how it will be measured. Specific metrics are presented that have a direct bearing on the performance issue. Current performance and the desired future performance are identified.

Returning to the case with FoodCo, specific customer service performance metrics were identified. These included first-time customer contact resolution and average customer order disposition time. Each of these metrics were tracked and reported on a weekly basis. Data showed that, during the time when customer service ratings slipped by almost 20%, first-time customer contact resolution dropped by 34%, while average customer order disposition time increased by 46%. The business case that the OD consultant prepared linked improvement of these two metrics to improved customer service ratings and linked improved customer service ratings to the business goal of revenue growth.

This analysis begs the next question of why performance has slipped so badly. This section concludes with a summary of the performance analysis. Supporting documentation, which can be considerable, is placed in the appendix. The performance analysis explains the root cause issues for the performance gap. The credibility of this analysis is enhanced by referencing the sources of the data. Often, verbal proofs or quotes from influential people are used (with their permission of course) to add credence to the conclusions of the analysis. Readers of the business case should have a clear understanding of the performance issue at this point, why this issue has surfaced, and how resolving this issue will help achieve the goals of the business.

Proposed Initiative

This section of the business case deals with what is being proposed to address the performance issue. The strategic change initiative is described in sufficient detail so that readers can understand what is being proposed and how it is expected to improve performance. The more detailed design of the initiative will come later, if the business leaders decide to move forward with the initiative. At this point the scope, timing, and boundaries of the initiative are defined. It is often effective to also state what the initiative is *not*. This helps crystallize in people's minds what to expect from the initiative and what not to expect. Think of this as inoculating the initiative from terminal scope creep. Drawing firm boundaries now will prevent the initiative from being drawn in too many directions later. Other boundaries to be explained include geography or company locations and/or specific business units, support units, or functions that will be included or excluded from the initiative.

In the FoodCo example, the initiative was broadly outlined in three phases: process redesign, restructuring the organization, and people development. This level of detail was sufficient to move the initiative forward and have the leaders commit to completing the detailed design of the initiative. The biggest challenge that the OD consultant faced was having these three initiative components addressed in the order he proposed. The diagnosis pointed to the buying process as the biggest culprit and the one that had to be addressed first. Next, the organization had to be restructured to support the new work process. Training sessions would follow to help people learn new behaviors and responsibilities.

Business Impact

For clients who are saying: "Show me the money!"—this is their section of the business case. Monetary benefits are estimated and the investment required to realize these benefits is presented. Generally, benefits are always presented before investments are outlined so that these investments can be placed in the perspective of achieving the benefits. Given all of the financial work that has been done to build the business case, estimating the financial benefits is fairly straightforward. The performance metrics are converted to monetary values and then a range of potential benefits is determined. For example, the two FoodCo metrics cited in an earlier section of the business case revealed that first-time customer contact resolution dropped by 34%, while average customer order disposition time increased by 46%. Standard values can be employed to calculate the monetary benefits that would be produced by bringing these two metrics back to previous performance levels. Benefits are always annualized, and one-time cost savings may be used in the business case;

however, one-time savings are not used in ROI calculations. Let's look at one of the FoodCo metrics as an example.

First-time customer contact resolution

Total customer contacts per month =	3121
Total first-time contacts resolved per month 2002 =	2878
Total first-time contacts resolved per month 2003 =	1899
Difference from 2002 to 2003 =	979
Standard value: added cost per contact =	$102
Cost of decreased performance per month =	$99,858
Annualized cost of decreased performance =	$1,198,296

This example shows that $1.2 million is being lost every year because of the customer service performance problem. The initiative is intended to recoup all of these monetary benefits. At this point the OD consultant can commit to achieving these benefits in one year after the deployment of the change initiative. Tracking mechanisms can be put in place to measure the financial gain to the business.

Note that there is no attempt here to isolate the effects of the initiative to produce these results. The magnitude of the FoodCo initiative was so great, and there was really no other initiative that could significantly affect this metric, so the client agreed to this approach. It is more often the case that clients expect only a portion of the performance metrics to be affected by the initiative, so benefits are estimated accordingly. For example, the FoodCo CEO could have expected the change initiative to improve performance as measured by this metric to be in the range of 50% to 80%. The $1.2 million would then be multiplied by these two percentages to create a range of expected benefits of $.6 million to $.96 million. Isolating the effects of an initiative on business performance is an extremely important issue. The following chapters show how to incorporate the isolation factor into the design and deployment of the initiative.

Readers of the business case have fixed their attention on the $1.2 million prize and are now ready to focus on the investment required to gain this prize. The OD consultant works with people in human resources, accounting, and other areas to determine the fully loaded costs for the initiative. These cost areas are outlined in detail in Chapter 7. Having in hand the monetary benefits and the cost data opens a couple of options for the business case. The first option is to forecast the ROI of the initiative. Forecasting ROI for strategic change initiatives is a powerful tool and is discussed in detail in Chapter 8. At this point, suffice it to say that forecasting ROI does require some assumptions to be made about the isolation factor and the conduct of initiative deployment. For example, with FoodCo, the cost of the initiative was estimated to be $320,000. Given an isolation factor of 50%, the benefits would be about $600,000. The forecasted ROI would be calculated as:

$$\text{ROI forecast} = ((\$600,000 - \$320,000) \div \$320,000) \times 100 = 87.5\%$$

When forecasting ROI, it is better to underpromise and overdeliver. The ROI of 87.5% represents a realistic forecast, especially because it is based on only one performance indicator. It should be noted that to most business leaders an ROI of 25% or greater is considered to be high, especially when compared to ROIs for other types of major business investments. ROIs for hard-asset improvement initiatives are generally in the range of 15% to 25%.

The second option that can be pursued is to develop a payback curve. The payback curve answers the question about when the monetary benefits will overtake the investments that have been made. (Chapter 5 presents a detailed example of how a payback curve can be constructed and utilized. Figure 5.1 graphically shows how a payback curve can be presented.) The client can provide guidance on whether there is a need for this type of calculation. It's really an issue about cash flow. Some strategic change initiatives are partially funded from the early financial benefits gained from the initiative. This represents a kind of pay-as-you-go approach, so it is important to post financial gains early in the project. If there is no pay, there is no go. In these cases, payback curves are essential because these calculations show how soon initiative investments are paid back. This information has a direct bearing on the potential balance sheet commitments the CEO has made.

Recommendations

The final section of the business case is the set of recommendations that the change practitioner makes to the CEO and other decision makers. The primary recommendation is to proceed with investing in the initiative. Sometimes the recommendation is only to proceed with the design of the initiative, and only when the design is complete will the decision be made whether to proceed with deployment. Recommendations can also be made about the scope and timing of the initiative. Governance of the initiative emerges at this point as a major issue. Recommendations should include how the initiative will be sponsored, managed, and measured. Governance bodies are often established to work through a myriad of issues related to the design, development, and deployment of the initiative. The next two chapters provide some examples about initiative governance.

The Business Case as a Tool of Change

The business case is a powerful and often overlooked tool to advance the cause of strategic change. Sharing all or part of the business case with others in the organization can generate good buzz and build momentum for change. Compile a list of leader and manager meetings, and schedule time in these meetings to share business case information. Demonstrate the monetary and intangible benefits that the initiative is expected to produce. Draw key messages from the business case and publish articles in company newsletters. Have the CEO featured in a short video about the change initiative and his or her commitment to see the change through. Investing in the business is always a positive message, and it is never too early to engage employees in the change effort.

CHAPTER 4

Design the Solution to Achieve Strategic Change Objectives

The client and key decision makers have agreed to advance the change initiative to the design phase. The consultant has his or her marching orders to design an initiative that will close the performance gap and contribute to achieving a top business goal. The consultant must now tap the talent of the organization to design the initiative in such a way that energizes people for strategic change. The seeds of success for deployment are planted during the design of the initiative. The first order of the day is to quickly establish a broad-based coalition for strategic change. This coalition will be the driving force for strategic change in the organization.

ORGANIZING A CHANGE COALITION

The client–consultant relationship that began during the diagnostic phase continues to grow and develop during the design phase. This relationship provides a foundation for others to be engaged with the initiative. An *ad hoc* change coalition is formed that engages the talent of the organization and the strategic change expertise of the consultant. This coalition will emerge as the team that is accountable for the overall success of the initiative and responsible for carrying out initiative activities. As the initiative progresses, more people are brought in to help, and as the coalition grows, specific roles and responsibilities emerge to meet the growing demands of executing the initiative. When the initiative is complete, the change coalition disbands.

The diversity of this coalition is the source of ideas, perspectives, and energy required for the strategic change to be successful. This diversity comes in many forms: business units and functions, geographic areas, product lines, organizational levels, cultural backgrounds, and many other forms. The coalition becomes, in effect, a microcosm of the greater organization. The representative nature of the coalition influences the shape, scope, and direction for strategic change.

Developing a Team Charter

Every team needs a game plan, and the change coalition is no different. A game plan helps each player know his or her responsibilities and what can be expected from the other players. The game plan also keeps players focused on the prize: what it will take to win. A team charter is the game plan for the change coalition. This charter outlines the team mission, objectives, key deliverables, responsibilities, and timing. The charter at this point in the process is focused on designing the change initiative. When (and if) the team is given the green light to proceed with developing the initiative, the team charter will be refreshed with a new challenge and new responsibilities.

The change coalition is dynamic and grows with the breadth, scope, and evolution of the change initiative. When initially formed, the change coalition typically consists of the client, who is also likely to be the sponsor of the initiative, the consultant, who is the lead change practitioner, and 10 to 12 other people who represent major facets of the organization. Table 4.1 describes these roles. As the initiative wends it way through development and deployment, the change coalition expands to meet these new challenges. Often, a formal governance body is empowered by the client to review and guide the work of the initiative. This governance body takes ownership for the success of the initiative. The change team is responsible for carrying out initiative activities. The ranks of the original 10 to 12 change team members swell as more talent and horsepower is required to move the initiative forward. Subgroups may be commissioned to complete specific tasks. Once these tasks are completed, the subgroups are disbanded.

Of course, people do not quit their day jobs when they sign on for additional duty with a change initiative. Participation in the change coalition is usually part-time and represents additional work that is piled on to people's day-to-day responsibilities. People engaged in this change effort have to learn how to wear two hats: their day-to-day functional job and their role on the change coalition. Conflicts inevitably occur as

Table 4.1 Roles of a Strategic Change Coalition

Role	Description
Client	The client owns the business issue. He or she has direct accountability to address this issue and has a personal stake in the success of the change initiative. In most cases the client also becomes the sponsor of the initiative.
Consultant	The consultant owns the change process. He or she has responsibility to develop and manage the change initiative following sound change management practices. In most cases the consultant is the lead change practitioner for the initiative.
Governance team	The governance team collectively owns the successful deployment of the initiative. Individually, as business unit and functional leaders, these team members are accountable for successful deployment in their respective organizations. Many, if not most, governance team members will organizationally report to the client and be part of the client's leadership team.
Change team	The change team owns the successful execution of all activities required to advance the initiative. At first, team direction comes from the client, and then later, from the governance team in the context of the team charter.
Subgroups	Subgroups own the successful execution of a specific task or activity. The life cycle of a subgroup is typically very short (two to six weeks).

priorities compete with each other. The consultant and client must be sensitive to these issues and structure and manage the change coalition so that people can wear their two hats as effectively as possible. The client and other leaders must be clear about the priorities they set for others. The consultant must ensure that people are organized optimally to achieve these priorities. Let's look at how one company, Antelope Energy, organized its change coalition to successfully execute a culture change initiative.

Building a Coalition for Change at Antelope Energy

Antelope Energy (a fictitious name), an independent U.S.-based oil exploration and production company, embarked on an ambitious culture

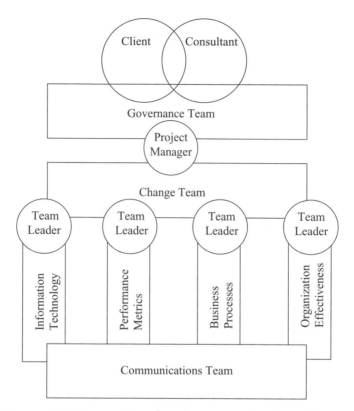

Figure 4.1 Organizing for change at Antelope Energy.

change initiative. This initiative included reengineering core work processes, realigning information systems to support these new work processes, and increasing the overall effectiveness of the organization. The CEO, who was the client for the initiative, knew that he needed to engage the hearts and minds of all employees in order for the culture change to be successful. He and his consultant organized an *ad hoc* change coalition to advance the culture change agenda in the organization. Figure 4.1 illustrates the structure of this coalition.

The client and consultant worked closely together in all aspects of the culture change effort. The CEO's direct reports, the consultant, and the (internal) project manager constituted the membership of the governance team. The project manager led the change team, which consisted of team leaders of the subgroups. Each subgroup was responsible for a particular aspect of the change initiative, including information technology, performance metrics, business processes, and organization effectiveness.

The organization effectiveness subgroup, for example, was responsible for training, development, leadership effectiveness, organization design, and human resources policies and procedures. The communications team was responsible for effective collaboration within the change coalition, communication within the entire organization, and community relations.

More than 100 people were ultimately tapped to play a role in the change coalition. Given the scope of the initiative—culture change—this level of resource commitment was appropriate. Creating a change coalition is a scalable process. Teams can be organized and charters written to appropriately match the scope of the strategic change effort. The larger the scope, the larger the change coalition will need to be. The client and the governance body decide on how best to structure and populate the change coalition.

Developing Strategic Change Objectives

Change initiatives become strategic when these initiatives directly impact business goals. It is critical, therefore, to explicitly link business goals with initiative objectives. Later, in Phase 3, evaluation objectives are in turn based on the initiative objectives. A line-of-sight linkage is created that integrates business goals, initiative objectives, and evaluation objectives. This linkage is the backbone of bottom-line OD. Without this linkage, strategic change cannot be effectively evaluated and understanding the business value of strategic change cannot be fully understood. Yet many change initiatives with aspirations of strategic impact are launched without completing this crucial step. In these cases, the linkage to the business goal is vague, based on the hope that people will take for granted that the change initiative will impact the business goal. The case of Braxton Industries illustrates this point.

CASE STUDY: DEVELOPING STRATEGIC CHANGE OBJECTIVES AT BRAXTON INDUSTRIES

The CEO at Braxton Industries (fictitious name) recognized that to achieve aggressive revenue growth goals there needed to be dramatic improvement in how people's performance was managed. An initiative was launched to revamp and deploy a consistent and effective performance management process throughout the company. Vendors were hired and the process design was launched. The initiative had the support of the CEO, and the emphasis was on speed: getting the initiative done quickly. The human resources leader threw a wrench into the mix. He directed that the initiative show a tangible return on investment. The initiative team was not clear about how to do this, so they turned to the project manager.

The project manager of the initiative brought in an evaluation expert to meet the wishes of the human resources leader. The project manager and the evaluator both quickly realized that the initiative objectives were not explicitly linked to the business goal of increasing revenue. The objectives that were written were limited by their focus on achieving *learning* outcomes and not taking the extra steps to focus on the achievement of *business* outcomes. For example, the objective of "learning the five-step relationship building process" spoke little to how this five-step process would be applied in the workplace and, if applied, how these new actions would affect revenue generation.

Expectations follow objectives, and for Braxton Industries this was a two-edged sword. First, if the change team did not set as an initiative objective the successful *application* of the process, then how can participants be expected to successfully apply the process to their work? The change team set its sights too low. Without ensuring application there can be little expectation that the initiative will have impact on the business. Design is geared toward achieving objectives. Consequently, activities that are more application focused—role plays, demonstrations, and the like—were not part of the original design because the original design was focused only on learning and not the application of learning. This brings us to the second edge of the sword. The vendors were delivering initiative materials based on learning-based objectives. Resetting the initiative objectives to focus on application and business objectives also meant that the project manager had to reset the expectations for what the vendors would deliver. The vendors had to include more experiential-based activities directed toward applying performance management skills for business benefit. This is not to say that learning-based objectives are not important because they are. It is just that learning-based objectives are not sufficient alone to drive the value of the initiative to have bottom-line business impact.

Together, the project manager and the evaluator developed strategic change objectives for the initiative and then developed evaluation objectives. Table 4.2 shows the fruits of their labors. The business goal was to grow annual revenue by 50% over the next five years. One of the performance management initiative objectives developed by the project manager and the evaluator was to achieve 10% higher performance from all salespeople and sales support staff through improved interactions. A link was made from higher performance of salespeople to increased

Table 4.2 Developing Objectives at Braxton Industries
Business Goal: Grow annual revenue by 50% over the next five years

Initiative Objective	Building Powerful Relationships Objective	Evaluation Objectives
Achieve 10% higher performance from all salespeople and sales support staff through improved interactions	Improved day-to-day interactions with increased collaboration and more effective communications by applying the five-step relationship-building process	Increased achievement of sales goals attributable to application of the five-step relationship-building process Increased productivity of sales support staff attributable to application of the five-step relationship-building process

revenue. In developing these objectives, they felt that it was important to break out the objectives of each subinitiative under the umbrella of the overall initiative of performance management. So, for example, one subinitiative was the Building Powerful Relationships series of workshops. As can be seen from Table 4.2, the objective from this subinitiative flows from the overall initiative objective: improved interactions will result from applying performance management skills. Two evaluation objectives were set: one based on sales performance for the salespeople and another based on increased productivity for the sales support staff. These evaluation objectives complete the clear line of sight to the business goal: growing revenue through improved interactions brought about by applying the five-step relationship-building process.

The Role of Governance in Developing Objectives

Given the critical importance of developing strategic objectives for the initiative, the client and governance team must approve these objectives and commit to achieving them. In the case of Braxton Industries, the project manager reviewed these objectives with the governance body, an advisory board for the initiative. This review was not only an opportunity to approve the objectives, but also an opportunity to educate the board members about how strategic change initiatives are evaluated. Consequently, the board began to accept this initiative as a *business* initiative and not just a human resources initiative. Gaining this kind of recognition and buy-in by these leaders is like money in the bank for when withdrawals are needed later to fund deployment. The leaders' commitment to deploying the initiative will reflect their commitment to improving the business and achieving the business goal.

DESIGNING THE STRATEGIC INITIATIVE

Form follows function, and in this case, design follows objectives. Designing an initiative geared toward business goals enables the initiative to have strategic impact. The design is guided by a set of design criteria. These criteria are based on people's expectations and the business requirements for how the initiative will solve the business issue at hand. The initiative, or solution, ultimately will be judged by how well it meets all of the stated criteria. This can be a tall order. Rapid prototyping has proven useful to effectively design strategic initiatives and to do so quickly and efficiently. When the design work is complete, a statement of work is drawn up that presents the proposed design of the solution, the benefits, and investments required. The client, and other governance bodies, approves the statement of work so that the initiative can proceed.

Develop Design Criteria

Design criteria represent the business requirements, leadership expectations, constraints, and limitations that must be addressed in the solution design. Figure 4.2 illustrates some design criteria for the performance management initiative. Business requirements are generally drawn directly from the business goal of the initiative. For example, the Braxton Industries goal of increasing sales revenue readily translates to a design criterion of "include managers of all product sales groups including sales support." Including all product sales groups will increase the ability of the initiative to affect sales. Leaders may have expectations regarding what the solution will look like. Braxton Industries leaders expected the new performance management initiative to incorporate the recently completed competency model. They also wanted the initiative to include best practices from the many different performance management processes that were in use throughout the company. These expectations were captured as design criteria.

Constraints represent those areas that cannot be changed by the initiative and are nonnegotiable. For example, the performance manage-

---

Design Criteria: Performance Management Initiative

1. Include managers of all product sales groups, including sales support.

2. Incorporate the new set of competencies developed for managers and leaders.

3. Include best-demonstrated practices from performance management processes currently in use worldwide.

4. Include a rating and ranking system that clearly differentiates performance levels.

5. Ensure that performance is evaluated annually and completed in the first quarter of every year.

6. Utilize available information systems and automation whenever possible to minimize administration and paperwork.

Figure 4.2 Design criteria.

ment initiative had to include a rating and ranking system and to evaluate performance on an annual basis. These were nonnegotiable items as far as the CEO and his leadership team was concerned. It was important for them to differentiate performance and to better coordinate performance management. Limitations generally refer to issues concerning resources. Information systems that do not consistently support people management processes throughout the world would be an example. A design criterion was included to maximize the use of available information systems. Later on, as the performance management process is developed and deployed, the information system limitations can be revisited. If these limitations are too onerous, recommendations can be made to upgrade the systems to better support performance management.

How can these expectations and constraints be navigated? Here is where the diverse nature of the change coalition can come to the rescue. The strength of the design criteria comes from how well these criteria meet the varied and diverse needs of the entire organization. The change coalition reflects this diversity and is therefore in a good position to craft criteria that will resonate with people in the organization. Typically, a formal interview protocol is drawn up, and each coalition team member fans out into the organization to conduct interviews. Leaders are interviewed, as are sales managers and sales consultants and a variety of others to gain a broader perspective. Coalition team members also contribute their own ideas to create a set of criteria. These criteria are presented to the client and governance bodies for review and approval.

Designing the Solution through Rapid Prototyping

The design criteria represent the formal link between the initiative objectives and the solution design. The next challenge is to quickly design the solution in a way that meets the needs of the business and gains the buy-in of the client and key constituents. Rapid prototyping has proven to be effective in designing strategic initiatives. Rapid prototyping is a kind of "fire, ready, aim" process. The intention is to produce workable drafts for review as quickly as possible. People, and especially senior leaders, are able to provide more insightful feedback more quickly when they have something tangible to bounce their ideas off of rather than staring at a blank sheet of paper.

There are four main steps in rapid prototyping, which are illustrated in Figure 4.3. The design criteria form the foundation for rapid prototyping. The change practitioner and others quickly translate the criteria into one or more workable solutions. It is a rare situation when one solution fully meets all of the design criteria. Some trade-offs are inevitable. A series of prototypes are produced that meet the design criteria to varying degrees. These prototypes are reviewed by a wide variety of people in focus groups. Functional reviews, regularly held leadership team meetings, and individual meetings with key constituents can also be conducted to review the prototypes. Gaining a diverse set of opinions at this juncture is important to rapidly advance the prototype process. Ownership of the prototype is increased as more fingers get put in the pie. People make contributions to develop the solution and as a result have increased ownership over the final product.

The change practitioner is on point to corral all of the opinions and feedback and use this information to design the advanced prototype. In many situations, more than one prototype will be designed, and in these cases it means going back to the focus groups. Thus another cycle of reviews and redesigns would be undertaken. This process is repeated as often as necessary to produce a final design for review. The client and

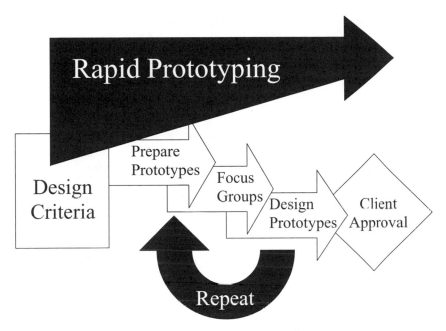

Figure 4.3 Rapid prototyping strategic change initiatives.

other governance bodies would then review and approve the final prototype. One consequence of this process is that it generates a lot of
excitement and enthusiasm for the initiative. People talk. Those people
who were in the focus groups will share their experiences with others
and expand their circle of enthusiasm for the initiative.

Writing the Statement of Work

Gaining approval on the design of the initiative does not guarantee client
approval to proceed with the initiative. Gaining client approval depends
on how well the client understands the business reason for the initiative,
what the initiative will accomplish, the financial and intangible benefits
it will produce, and what resources will be required to achieve these benefits. The statement of work addresses each of these areas.

The statement of work can take many forms—anything from a short
letter to the client to a binder-sized document. The intention of the statement of work is to create a kind of bill of goods for the client so that
everyone is clear what the initiative will and will not do. Some of this
material can be based on what was presented in the business case. In
general, the statement of work should include the following:

- ☐ An *executive summary* that succinctly summarizes the document

- ☐ A *background statement* that presents the business need for the initiative; this material may be drawn from the business case.

- ☐ The *solution description* that summarizes the design criteria and how the initiative design meets these criteria

- ☐ An *evaluation component* that outlines how the initiative will be evaluated, including the initiative objectives; these objectives are linked to the business goals.

- ☐ *Benefits* that state the financial and intangible benefits expected from the initiative; an ROI forecast, if completed, can be presented here.

- ☐ A *project plan overview*, including major activities, timing, and deliverables; this is often presented as a Gantt chart that serves as a weekly project management tool.

- ☐ An *investment summary* that shows what money, people, and time will be required to successfully deploy the initiative

The statement of work can serve as a useful communication tool. The change practitioner can prepare an early discussion draft of the document and review this document with several key constituents before submitting the document to the client for review and decision. These constituents will offer insightful ideas and comments that can be incorporated into the final document. Not only will this process improve the quality of the final draft submitted to the client, but it will also continue to build ownership and buy-in by these key constituents to the final initiative design.

This statement of work will also be referred to several times during the course of the initiative. Many questions will arise during the initiative about what may be in or out of the scope of the initiative. Referring to the statement of work helps answer these questions and limit scope creep. The statement of work is also useful for bringing new project team members onboard, developing key messages to communicate to the organization, and supporting project decisions along the way. For example, decisions about selecting deployment options can be supported by reviewing the statement of work and refreshing people's minds about the original commitments they made.

CHAPTER 5

Develop a Change Plan with Evaluation Objectives

CHANGE MANAGEMENT AND EVALUATION: OPENING DOORS TO UNDERSTANDING

When planning a strategic change initiative, it is never too early to think about evaluation. Developing a change management plan requires many decisions to be made about the timing of deployment activities, the sequence of business units or functions that will be involved in the deployment, and the scope of the deployment. These decisions have implications for how the change initiative can be evaluated. More important, building evaluation activities into the change plan opens new doors to understanding—and increasing—the value of the change for the business. Developing the change plan and the evaluation plan together optimizes the value of both.

Let's get to the crux of the issue: isolation. Understanding how the change initiative adds value to the organization requires that the effects of the change initiative be reasonably isolated from all other potential influences. We say reasonably isolated because this is not an exact science. Judgments are made. Estimations are taken. More than 80 years of empirical research in the social and behavioral sciences provide tried-and-true evaluation methodology that can be adapted to isolating the effects of a change initiative. For more than 20 years, pioneers like Jack Phillips have adapted evaluation methodology to a variety of training and human resource development programs. It is high time to routinely extend this methodology to strategic change initiatives.

Later in this chapter we talk about various strategies to isolate the effects of the change initiative. Optimizing these strategies will be done through the decisions made in conjunction with the change management plan. For example, the timing of the deployment activities can better position pre-/post-initiative analysis of the data and open ways to look at how the initiative may have influenced trends in performance. Managing the sequence of engaging business units or functions in the initiative opens new possibilities for comparison (or control) groups to be used in the isolation effort. Decisions about the overall scope of the initiative (e.g., deploy in sales and marketing but not in manufacturing) have implications for the kinds of effects to be isolated (e.g., look at revenue margins but not warranty costs).

Integrating evaluation and change management is not done just for the convenience of evaluation. The ability of the organization's leaders to better manage the change process is greatly enhanced. Progress on achieving the organization goals can be better tracked. Evaluation objectives have a direct bearing on the initiative objectives, and success achieving the initiative objectives bodes well for achieving the organization goals. Tracking these performance data and providing timely progress updates improves decision making by the client and governance bodies. Midcourse corrections can be taken based on data, not suppositions. In this way, evaluation brings into focus the outcomes (what) of change as well as the process (how) of managing change. It is clear that evaluation cannot be an afterthought to the change management plan.

ELEMENTS OF AN EFFECTIVE CHANGE PLAN

Bottom-line OD raises the bar of acceptability for approaches to change management. Certain disciplines must be put into place. Although there are many well-documented approaches to change management, bottom-line OD requires change management plans to have certain ingredients. The processes and practices of bottom-line OD can be integrated into any change management approach, given that these ingredients are present. If these ingredients are not present in the change management approach, then these ingredients must be added or another approach to change management must be adopted.

There are five essential ingredients that bottom-line OD requires for change management:

1. *The change management plan must be geared toward accomplishing stated business objectives.* Vague pronouncements of how the initiative is connected to the business goal are not sufficient. The explicit links from the business goal to the initiative objective

and from the initiative objective to the evaluation objectives are central to bottom-line OD.

2. *Initiative deployment is utilized to improve the quality of evaluation.* Many aspects of deployment have a direct bearing on evaluation activities. The use of pilots, the sequencing, and the timing of the deployment throughout an organization offer opportunities to isolate the effects of the initiative and to better understand the impact that the initiative has on the business.

3. *Sponsorship for the initiative is clearly defined.* The implementation of bottom-line OD is geared toward the client, sponsor (if a different person than the client), and the governance bodies. Evaluation data improve these individuals' ability to make decisions and manage the initiative for maximum strategic impact.

4. *Strategic communications are utilized.* Communication is viewed as a strategic change tool in its own right, preparing the organization for change and providing feedback and recognition on the progress of the change. The evaluation provides critical information that can be used to craft key messages about the business value of the initiative. Key messages can include findings from the evaluation that can further the cause of engaging people and recognizing their efforts to make the change successful.

5. *The change plan is dynamic.* The change plan will feature periodic opportunities for leaders to take stock of what is and what is not working well. Evaluation data can provide insights into progress and suggest improvement actions. The leaders, then, are in a better position to take any needed corrective action steps.

Elements of an Effective Evaluation Plan

Although the change plan represents the architecture for successfully deploying strategic change, the evaluation plan captures the essence of how success of the strategic change will be measured. There are four major elements of an evaluation plan:

1. Evaluation objectives
2. Evaluation approach
3. Sources of value
4. Data collection plan

Each of these elements is discussed in detail, and selected case study examples are used to illustrate how these elements are developed.

Evaluation Objectives

Evaluation objectives are the heart of the evaluation plan. These objectives form the basis of how the success of the initiative will be determined. There are up to five levels at which these objectives are established. Selecting the appropriate level or levels for the evaluation objectives depends on the initiative objective. There are some specific ways in which the most appropriate evaluation objectives are matched with the initiative objective. This is a critically important activity, and, in many cases, this matching process highlights inadequacies with the way in which initiative objectives are written. It is important, therefore, to understand the characteristics of well-written and poorly written objectives. Each of these issues is explored in detail.

Five Levels of Evaluation Objectives

There are five distinct levels of evaluation. One or more objectives are typically developed for each of these levels. Table 5.1 defines these five levels. Each of these levels builds on each other up to level 5, ROI. Not every strategic change initiative will be evaluated at level 5 and possibly not even at level 4. For example, the business impact of some change initiatives may be so long term that it is not feasible to evaluate the impact. Warranty cost improvements generated by an initiative may take years to materialize. So not all levels of analysis will be used in all cases; however, whatever the highest level of evaluation is for an initiative, it is important to collect data at each of the lower levels. For example, an initiative that was evaluated at level 4, business results, would also be evaluated at lower levels (e.g., levels 1, 2, and 3). This approach is taken, in part, to help build a story about how the initiative is changing the hearts (reaction) and minds (learning) of people to adopt new behavior in the workplace (application) that creates lasting value (business results).

People in different roles will tend to have greater or lesser interest in the outcomes of the evaluations at each level. Leaders will tend to be most interested in data from level 3 and above. They will want to see changes in behavior (level 3) and business performance (level 4). Leaders will also be keenly interested if the cost to produce these benefits was justified, given the benefits (level 5). Change practitioners and facilitators will at first be interested in the early returns of the evaluation gained primarily from data at levels 1 and 2. These early returns suggest what is going well and what, if anything, the change practitioners and

Table 5.1 Definitions of the Five Levels of Evaluation

Level	Title	Description for Strategic Change Initiatives
1	Reaction	Early reaction of the participants to the change initiative. Areas of interest include relevance of the initiative to address the problem at hand, assessment of the ability of people to carry out the initiative, how well prepared the organization is for change.
2	Learning	What the participants are learning from the initiative. Areas of interest include how well participants understand their new roles and responsibilities, how the initiative is expected to improve organization performance, potential barriers or problems they foresee with application.
3	Application	How effectively the participants are applying the new tools and knowledge gained from the initiative. Areas of interest include what participants are doing differently as a result of the initiative, what impact these new actions are having on their work performance.
4	Business results	The impact of the initiative on organization performance. This impact is isolated from all other potential influences on organization performance. Impact effects are converted to monetary value. Results can also be expressed as intangible benefits, and these intangibles often complement the monetary benefits.
5	Return on investment	The return on investment that the initiative contributes to the business. The total monetary investment made in the initiative is tabulated and factored into ROI and benefits/cost ratio calculations.

facilitators need to do to improve the rollout of the initiative. Later on, as the deployment concludes, everyone becomes keenly interested in the business results and ROI.

Matching Evaluation Objectives with Initiative Objectives

The highest level of evaluation is generally limited to the highest-level objectives set by the initiative. For example, setting the initiative objective at level 2 generally limits the ability to evaluate at a higher level. If the initiative was not intended to deliver results above a level 2, then why evaluate the initiative above this level? Unfortunately, the answer often is that the initiative was expected to deliver business results, but the objectives were never calibrated accordingly. This was the situation with setting objectives for the performance management initiative at Braxton Industries illustrated in Chapter 4. Fortunately, in this example, the mismatch between initiative objective and business outcome was detected early. Much more challenging is when this kind of situation presents itself after deployment. When the mismatch between the level of the initiative objective and the leaders' expectation of value does not come to light until the initiative has been deployed it is too late to do anything differently with the initiative. This all too common situation underscores the importance of appropriately setting objectives for the change initiative. Chapter 10 provides some strategies for recovering from this unfortunate set of circumstances.

To illustrate this point, an OD manager contracted an evaluation specialist to conduct an ROI study on a recently completed strategic initiative. This initiative involved deploying a change management process throughout a business unit. Deployment included change management workshops followed up with team coaching sessions. Informal comments made by participants were mixed: good content, but the change management process still seemed too academic. The business unit vice president got wind of these comments and was concerned about gaining the expected value of the change management initiative to the business.

Examining the objectives and deployment of the initiative revealed the following chronology of decisions and actions:

- [ ] Initiative objectives were limited to level 2 learning, for example:
    - [ ] "Understand the five-step change management process."
    - [ ] "Gain insights into how to apply change management."
    - [ ] "Identify the top seven causes of resistance to change."

- [ ] Change management workshops were geared to accomplish these objectives and, therefore, did not emphasize application of the change management process to the work environment.
    - [ ] Case studies were used to illustrate concepts and how change management was used by other organizations. The workshop did not take the next step of having participants apply their learnings to their own change management challenges.
    - [ ] Action learning, whereby participants would be able to work with others on real-life issues, was not used in the workshops, nor was any other type of experiential learning used.

☐ Application of change management to real business issues was left to the team coaching sessions, but these sessions occurred several weeks after the workshops had been completed, at which point frustration and skepticism had crept in. This time lag was too great for people to make the leap from theory to practical application. The credibility of the OD team had suffered as a consequence.

The evaluation specialist did not proceed with the ROI study at that time, but rather recommended that the six members of the vice president's leadership team each work with an OD consultant on a critical and current business issue utilizing change management. Each of these six projects incorporated evaluation methodology to ensure that level 5 ROI objectives would be set and actions taken to achieve these objectives. Implementing the ROI process focused these leaders on addressing a business issue and, in so doing, pointed the way to create added value in their respective organizations.

The bottom line is that it is recommended that objectives for strategic change initiatives be set at level 4 (business results) or level 5 (ROI). Change becomes strategic when it affects the strategic goals of the business. Making the link from initiative objective to business goal requires setting level 4 or level 5 as the target. In some cases, setting a strategic change objective at level 3 may be appropriate, but this should be the exception rather than the rule. People may successfully apply the tools and knowledge of an initiative but still not have any appreciable impact on the business.

Elements of a Good Evaluation Objective

What makes a good evaluation objective for a change initiative? There are three elements: attribution, direction, and relevance.

☐ *Attribution*. The expected change in performance is largely a result of the initiative, although other factors may be involved. The topic of how the effects of the initiative are isolated from these other factors is discussed later in this chapter.

☐ *Direction*. The objective states what will increase (e.g., sales) or decrease (e.g., costs). If specific targets are set, then include these targets in the objective as well.

☐ *Relevance*. The objective must relate to a strategic business goal. Often these are the top five to ten goals of the business. If these goals are not articulated for the business, the evaluation objective must relate to some aspect of the organization's strategy (e.g., increased market share).

For example, Braxton Industries set as an evaluation objective for the performance management initiative "increased achievement of sales goals attributable to application of the five-step relationship-building process." Breaking this objective down we see that:

Direction   Increased

Relevance   Sales goals are key to the business goal of increasing revenue by 50% over the next five years.

Attribution   Attributable to application of the five-step relationship-building process, which suggests that these effects will have to be isolated from the effects of other influences. It is reasonable that better managing the performance of salespeople will increase sales, which will help achieve the business goals.

The Costs of Using Poorly Defined Evaluation Objectives

Much of the evaluation architecture is structured around the evaluation objectives. Poorly defined objectives limit understanding the business impact of a change initiative and carry other significant costs. Here are some of the most costly consequences of developing and using poorly defined evaluation objectives:

☐ *Deployment of the initiative that is geared toward inappropriate objectives is doomed to fail or at least be perceived to fail.* As we saw in the case of the change management initiative, objectives set and later evaluated at level 2 (learning) did not capture the full benefits expected by the business unit VP. The evaluation specialist ended up sending the OD manager back to the drawing board to revamp the change management initiative.

☐ *Expectations of the sponsor and senior leaders for the results of the initiative will likely not be met.* Leaders manage what they measure, and mismeasurement leads to mismanagement. When evaluation objectives do not connect with initiative objectives, evaluating the results of the initiative will be misleading and will likely not meet the leaders' expectations.

☐ *Resources will be underutilized.* People will not be focused on the higher-priority activities, and investment decisions will be made that will not optimize the effectiveness of the initiative. Rework will be created. Returning again to the change management example, the initial change management workshops did not hit their mark and had to be partially repeated by each of the VP's leadership team members. Although the end result was very effective, the team members did not use their resources wisely to get to the end result.

☐ *The organization risks not meeting its performance objectives.* The reason for launching the change initiative in the first place was to improve business performance in some significant ways. Suboptimizing the initiative suboptimizes the achievement of the performance objectives.

☐ *There are opportunity costs: products are not developed, production is lost, and sales are not captured.* Again in the change management example, the organization lost valuable time by not implementing change management sooner. The six change management teams that were launched achieved significant benefits, but the delay in launching these teams delayed achieving these benefits. This represented a missed opportunity for the business.

Rules of Thumb for Developing Evaluation Objectives

When developing evaluation objectives, less is definitely more. A considerable amount of effort is required to evaluate each objective, so a liberal dose of common sense is called for. Choices have to be made that balance the need to know with the expenditure of money and resources to produce the knowledge. Here are three proven rules of thumb for developing evaluation objectives:

1. *Develop no more than two or three objectives for each evaluation level.* A change initiative may have several objectives. Do not feel that every one of these initiative objectives must be evaluated. Select only the top two or three. Pick your battles; each objective requires time and effort to evaluate.

2. *Work with the client and governance bodies to determine which objectives are most valuable.* In so doing, the client and governance bodies are also expressing their views on what they most value from the initiative. Their buy-in to the evaluation objectives increases as a result of helping determine these objectives.

3. *Keep the objectives short—no more than 15 or so words.* A lengthy objective may be an indication of a lack of precision about the expected outcomes of the initiative. It may also be an indication that one objective is really two objectives. If this is the case, these two objectives must be broken apart to become stand-alone objectives. Please refer to Table 4.2 to review two examples of evaluation objectives.

Sources of Value

Now that you have nailed down the evaluation objectives, you are prepared for the next step of identifying specific sources of value. Value can be either tangible or intangible. This chapter—and for that matter, this book—focuses on tangible value and converting this value into monetary benefits. This focus is not intended to diminish the importance of intangible value, however, because intangible value can be the most important source of benefits for a strategic change initiative. OD practitioners have generally concentrated on extolling to their clients the intangible value gained from their initiatives. The big challenge for us all is to make the intangible tangible: to document the tangible value that the strategic change initiative creates for the business.

FOUR CATEGORIES OF TANGIBLE VALUE

There are four major categories of tangible value: output, quality, time, and cost. Table 5.2 defines these four categories. Identifying the particular source or sources of value for a strategic change initiative begins with the evaluation objective. It is usually not possible or appropriate to measure all of the potential sources of value for an initiative. The cost of evaluation would climb to unacceptable levels. Therefore, trade-offs must be made. The evaluation objectives point the way toward knowing what is most important to be measured.

Let's illustrate this point with an example. A product line business unit leader at Braxton Industries set as an evaluation objective the increased achievement of sales goals attributable to the performance management initiative. The benefit source was identified as an output, specifically, revenue incremental to sales goals achieved by salespeople. The business leaders expressed confidence that the sales force would achieve their sales targets for the year without the managers participating in the performance management initiative. These leaders did concede that a portion of the revenue produced that was *incremental* to these

Table 5.2 Definitions of the Four Major Categories of Tangible Value

Category	Definition	Examples
Output	The number of units (or monetary value of the units) produced within a certain period	The number of customer call resolutions per hour The revenue margins produced by the Western region each period
Quality	The number of units (or monetary value of the units) produced that do not meet specifications	The number of assembly-related defects for a product line The warranty cost incurred within 200 hours of product use
Time	The speed at which a product or service is developed, produced, or distributed	The number of days required to develop a new product The average number of days to complete a project mission
Cost	The amount of money required to produce units or deliver services	The average manufacturing cost to produce a given product The average cost per transaction to deliver customer service in a call center

goals could be attributed to improved performance management. Two considerations were surfaced: (1) that only margins would be considered as benefits (not gross revenue), and (2) the impact of the performance management initiative on incremental revenue would have to be isolated from other potential factors.

Some readers might be suspicious with this example that the "fix was in." In other words, the business unit leader seemed skeptical that the performance management initiative would be valuable for the sales force. Only including as benefits margins on an isolated portion of *incremental* revenue ensures deep discounts in the benefits total, especially after the discounts for contribution factors and error factors are taken into account. For example, if the total revenue increase is $18 million, taking all of these considerations into account yields total benefits of only $48,960.

Total revenue increase =	$18,000,000
Revenue incremental to goals =	$4,000,000
Margins (net revenue) × 12% =	$480,000
Contribution (isolation) factor × 17% =	$81,600
Confidence (error) factor × 60% =	$48,960

Initiative costs are likely to be higher than $50,000, in fact, several times this amount. It does not look good for a robust ROI, so what's an evaluator to do? One approach to take is to look for other sources of value. Another output measure, productivity, would be a likely candidate. A reasonable case could be made that improving performance would also improve productivity. The evaluator, change practitioner, client, and others could get together and devise a reasonable approach to include productivity in the evaluation. A valid point could be made that adding the productivity measure would provide a more complete picture of the full benefits of the initiative.

Up to this point we have talked about monetary benefits as if there was just one kind. In fact, there are three major types of monetary benefits:

1. *Annualized benefits.* These benefits are produced at a rate that is then calculated for a 12-month period. These benefits are sustainable for a period of years. Annualized benefits are used in ROI calculations.

2. *One-time benefits.* These benefits are produced once and only once (e.g., a one-time inventory reduction). These benefits are not used for ROI calculations.

3. *In-pocket benefits.* These benefits refer to cash produced by the initiative within the fiscal year that the initiative was deployed.

For the most part, this book focuses on the first type, annualized benefits. The second type, one-time benefits, is not used in the ROI analysis. The third type, in-pocket benefits, are a kind of hybrid and can fall into either of the other two camps. In-pocket benefits (also called "green dollars") are those benefits that are produced in the same year that the costs are incurred. If these are annualized benefits (say, dollars gained from increased sales), then these can be included in the ROI analysis. If these are one-time benefits (say, selling fixed assets that will no longer be needed), then these are not included in the ROI analysis. Just because these benefits are not included in the ROI analysis, however, does not mean that they are not important. Clients may need this additional source of cash to fund the initiative!

Some initiatives may be unfunded or underfunded with the expectation that the initiative will pay back on the investment in time to pay for some of the bills incurved by the initiative. Payback charts may be established to estimate and track how soon the monetary benefits will have covered the initial cost of the initiative. For some clients this issue

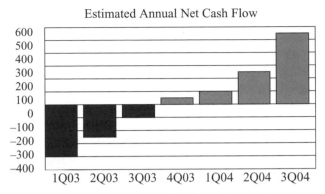

Figure 5.1 Example of a payback chart for a change initiative.

can be important, especially if their neck is on the line to meet financial obligations. Figure 5.1 illustrates a payback chart for an initiative. By reading this chart it can be seen that the brunt of the cost of the initiative will be incurred in the first quarter of 2003. As the benefits from the initiative kick in, the cost of the initiative is reduced. Actually, the net quarterly cash flow picture improves. The situation looks positively rosy by the end of 2003, with the cash flow becoming positive. By the end of 2004 the initiative is generating a positive cash flow of more than $500,000. A CEO will love this schedule, especially because the cost outlay of the initiative is covered within the year of investment, 2003.

This chart presents an elegant way of portraying financial benefits. (It also suggests when to calculate the ROI!) This picture can get complex very quickly, however. The CFO may raise some additional considerations. These are presented so that readers are at least aware that the client may have other requirements for reporting benefits. If any of these issues are raised, reach for the aspirin and contact your local accountant.

☐ *Amortization.* Larger investments are often spread out over a period of time. Some organizations may view part of the investment in a change initiative to be large enough to amortize over several years. Software and hardware, for example, may be amortized over several years. In this case, only one-third of the total expenditure of the hardware and software for an initiative would be included in the ROI analysis. This is because only one year of (annualized) benefits are used in the ROI calculation and so it is important to compare one year of cost with one year of benefits.

☐ *Cost of money.* This consideration may hit the cost side or the benefit side of the ROI equation. In terms of cost, some organizations levy an additional charge to initiative teams based on what it costs the corporation to borrow money. This charge is typically about 10% per year. So, in this case, the entire annual budget of the initiative would be multiplied by 10%, and this added cost would factor into the ROI equation. It's like the organization was saying to the initiative leaders, "Look, we had to pay a 10% fee to give you this money and we're passing that fee on to you." In terms of applying the cost of money factor to benefits, the organization may subtract 10% of the investment money from the initiative benefits on the grounds that this money is would have been earned anyway (by investing the money in something else) without the initiative. If the cost of money consideration is taken, it should be assessed on either the cost side or the benefits side, but not both.

☐ *Economic value added (EVA).* The recent trend of focusing on EVA financial results introduces a higher bar for investment benefits of business initiatives. According to EVA, investments must perform significantly higher than the cost of money or the investments are withdrawn. Over time, lower value-added activities are dropped, leaving the business with only the higher performing activities. People and change initiatives usually fall under the EVA radar screen, although business leaders are increasingly holding these initiatives to the same standards as other business initiatives.

☐ *After-tax cash flow.* This consideration takes into account tax liability and reduces the benefits accordingly. Corporate taxes are amazingly complex and fluctuate quite a bit. These tax rates can be as high as 23% to 35%, which represent a significant discount of the benefits. In effect, this means that the initiative leaders have to "pay taxes" on the benefits the initiative produced before calculating the ROI.

☐ *Net present value.* This consideration is based on the idea that a dollar today is worth more than a dollar next year. Net present value represents a different kind of ROI. It's a way of expressing a future ROI in present dollar terms. Briefly, the ROI would be projected out over time, and discount factors would be applied to the ROI to bring it back to what the ROI would be in present dollars. The ROI is balanced against several risk factors and assumptions that are made about when the money would materialize. Each year in the future has a slightly different discount rate. The organization will have standard values for the discounts.

☐ *Margins on sales revenues*. Benefits are rarely based on total revenue increases; rather the sales margins are used. Margins may vary by product or service, and the organization should have captured these margins as standard values. Typically, product margins are in the 5% to 20% range, with margins for services a bit higher, usually in the 15% to 40% range. Often, clients will offer a range of margins for products and services. In these cases it is best to be conservative and select the lowest margin value offered within the range for the ROI calculations.

☐ *Currency conversion*. Initiatives that involve two or more countries must account for currency fluctuations. Currency rates fluctuate quite a bit, so benefits and costs have to take these fluxuations into account. Often, in-country benefits are determined as well as those converted to a common currency, usually U.S. dollars. Both in-country and U.S. converted monetary benefits can be used in ROI calculations. Comparing in-country costs with in-country benefits yields an accurate portrayal of ROI. The wrinkle here is when the funding source is in U.S. dollars and the benefits are expressed in another currency. It is really up to the client to make the best call that will yield the most accurate portrayal of the benefits of an initiative. Whatever approach is taken, it should apply to both costs and benefits alike.

Fishing Expeditions

All of the foregoing discussion on the sources of value assumes that these sources are known at the beginning of the analysis. This is not always the case. To some extent fishing expeditions are allowed. After all, every ROI study is an experiment and an exploration into the unknown. Being open to understanding the impact of an initiative requires transcending preconceived notions about the value that the initiative may or may not be creating. This is especially true when few previous studies are available for comparison.

A great example of this situation comes from Chapter 11, the case study on executive coaching. When a company asked an evaluator to conduct an ROI study on executive coaching, there were no previous coaching ROI studies to build on. In this case, the evaluator probed all conceivable sources of potential benefits. The results showed that some sources, such as productivity, were more potent than other sources. Subsequent ROI studies on coaching can build on these findings to focus data collection on the benefit sources with the greatest potential to produce monetary benefits.

Data Collection Plan

The final step in the process of developing the evaluation plan is to show how the data will be collected for all relevant evaluation levels both during and after the initiative deployment. Once again, the less is more rule is apt. Let's start with the example shown in Table 5.3. This data collection plan for Braxton Industries includes evaluation levels, evaluation objectives, evaluation methods, timing, and responsibilities. The performance management initiative is expected to deliver business results, specifically, increased achievement of sales goals attributable to performance management. Evaluating the initiative at this level (4) also requires evaluation at lower levels (1–3). The objectives for these lower levels are presented as well. The methods refer to the specific way in which data will be collected. This plan utilizes questionnaires, tests, observations, and report reviews for each of the four levels of data, respectively. The timing of the administration for the data gathering is specified. Data collection responsibilities are identified for each level of data required. Workshop facilitators, sales managers, human resources managers, the finance department, and the evaluator all have important parts to play in collecting data.

The guiding rule in developing a data collection plan is to provide just enough information so that those who are responsible for an evaluation activity can accomplish the activity successfully. Providing too many instructions may obfuscate their responsibilities to collect the data. Of course, this plan may be augmented by those responsible for carrying out the plan. They may wish to detail the specific actions that the evaluation will require. For example, assessing the level 3 application data required direct observations of the sales managers working with three of their salespeople. Some specific actions required to make this happen include developing an observation protocol, developing scripts for the sales manager and human resources manager to explain this process to the sales force, and developing a tracking mechanism to record the timing of each performance discussion. The people who carry out the plan are empowered to use their best judgment about how to do so.

Table 5.3 Example of Data Collection Plan for Braxton Industries

Level	Objectives	Methods	Timing	Responsibility
1 Reaction	PM perceived as relevant to improving performance of salespeople	Workshop questionnaire	Completed by all workshop participants at the end of the workshop	Workshop facilitators
2 Learning	Understand new performance management process	Test for comprehension	Completed by all workshop participants at the end of the workshop	Workshop facilitators
3 Application	Successfully conduct new performance management process with three salespeople	Direct observation	Completed within three weeks of workshop completion	Sales manager and human resources manager
4 Business Results	Increased achievement of sales goals attributable to performance management	Review of monthly sales reports	Base period = six months before initiative deployment Test period = every month for 12 months after initiative deployment	Business unit finance department and initiative evaluator

There are two final considerations for the data collection plan. The first consideration is to be sensitive to the ease with which people can access the data. Often there are multiple systems and data-keeping mechanisms, some of which are easier to work with than others. Some business units or functions keep their own set of books (sometimes unofficially) with specialized performance data and unique indicators that they use for their business. Personnel data may be kept on a series of spreadsheets. The evaluation is faced with a situation in which these various systems rarely talk to each other, complicating the access to data. Enterprise Resource Planning (ERP) systems have made inroads in the collection and management of a common set of data, but much progress still has to be made, especially when dealing with people-related data.

The second consideration is to incorporate the data collection—and for that matter, the evaluation planning activities—into the overall initiative project plan. There really should be only one change plan and not two separate plans, one for evaluation and one for change, because having one plan emphasizes the integration of evaluation and change management. Everyone leading and working with the initiative has a vested interest in seeing both kinds of activities completed successfully. Another reason for having one change plan is that this integration of activities enables the initiative project manager to better track the evaluation progress in the context of the other initiative activities. Off-schedule conditions become apparent sooner, and resource utilization can be optimized for everyone. In the lingo of the project manager, evaluation and change activities are interdependent with multiple examples of antecedents and consequences.

ISOLATING THE EFFECTS OF THE INITIATIVE

The Paradox: Making the Intangible Tangible

Strategic change is comprehensive and long lasting. Strategic change initiatives typically cover the entire organization and make profound changes in one or more business processes or organization capabilities. Three examples can be found in Section Three of this book: (1) executive coaching was used to accelerate the development of leaders; (2) organization capability alignment was used to drive the organization strategically; and (3) knowledge management created a companywide capability to continuously leverage knowledge. The benefits of these initiatives are intended to be experienced for many years after the initiatives have completed. Leaders continue to improve their businesses; the strategic alignment of the organization is sustainable; and leveraging knowledge continues into the foreseeable future.

Paradoxically, these very qualities of continuous and long-lasting value make isolating the effects of a strategic change initiative more challenging. Note the primary benefits of these initiatives—leadership, strategic alignment, and leveraging knowledge. These are intangible benefits, which are not easily given to quantitative analysis. Yet, in each of these cases, tangible monetary benefits were identified and the effects of the initiative to create these monetary benefits were isolated. Accomplishing this task of isolating benefits requires choices to be made, like what will and will not be measured. Not everything can be measured, and not even some of the most important benefits can be measured. Unmeasured benefits remain intangible, and yet play an important part in understanding the strategic value of an initiative. Tangible and intangible benefits are not mutually exclusive. In fact, they are two sides of the same coin. Both are required to gain a glimpse of the true picture of how a change initiative adds value to the organization.

Critical Considerations for Isolating the Effects

Effectively isolating the effects of a strategic initiative requires that we pick our battles carefully. Choices must be made about what to measure and what will remain intangible. There are four critical considerations for making these choices and isolating the effects of the initiative:

1. *You can't measure everything, so measure what's truly important.* The ROI is never based on all benefits, only those benefits that are deemed most important to capture. Make sure that what you are measuring will have meaning for the client and governance bodies and that it passes your test of common sense.

2. *Understand all of the other potential influences on performance, both within and outside of the organization.* Each of these potential influences may be perceived as affecting the key performance variables. Note these influences and enter them into the isolation equation. For example, when estimating the impact of the initiative on performance, also estimate the impact of these other influences. Given that these estimates will total 100%, a gain in one influencing factor may come at the expense of the estimated impact of the initiative. Although this approach reduces the mon-

etary benefits of the change initiative, it does produce a more credible analysis in the eyes of others.

Let's return briefly to the example of the business leaders who believed that only a portion of incremental sales revenue would result from the performance management initiative. The evaluator could ask the business leaders about other potential influences. Let's say that they add two: the new compensation plan and the high quality of sales leadership. Given this response, the evaluator can isolate the effects of these two influencing factors along with the performance management initiative. This approach would provide a more complete and more credible picture of the impact of the initiative on the business.

3. *Build a case for the cause and effect.* Stories that show how the initiative affected performance can be a powerful way to build a case that the change initiative had impact. The data drawn from levels 1 through 4 can be helpful as source data to write these stories. For example, learning about how someone creatively applied new performance management tools to increase the sales performance of her team can be written about in story form (with her permission, of course). These stories illustrate in practical, nononsense terms how the change initiative affected the business. The use of multiple isolation methods reinforces the case for cause and effect. There are three primary isolation strategies, which are discussed in detail in the next section.

4. *Manage the credibility of the analysis.* Be aware that the analysis is only as credible as the process followed and the people conducting it. Chapter 7 offers some helpful guidelines in how to build credibility for the analysis. Figure 7.1 illustrates these guidelines. The point to be made here is that the change practitioner must be aware that credibility is a serious issue and that it is his or her responsibility to effectively manage this issue.

Strategies for Isolating the Effects of Strategic Change

Strategic change places special challenges on isolating its effects on performance. This is perhaps one reason why so little has been done to date to isolate these effects. In any event, three major strategies have emerged to isolate the effects of strategic change: pre-/post-initiative

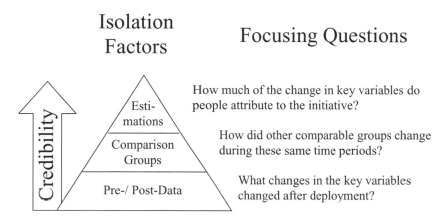

Figure 5.2 Strategies to isolate the effects of the change initiative.

analysis, comparison groups, and estimation. The client, change practitioner, governance bodies, and others must decide on the most appropriate isolation strategy during the development phase of the initiative. This task is appropriate at this point because decisions are made about timing, sequencing, and scope during the development phase. Timing has a direct bearing on how (or if) a pre-/post-initiative analysis can be used, and sequencing has implications for identifying possible comparison groups.

Think of these strategies as building blocks (Figure 5.2). The more of these building blocks that are used, the stronger the resulting structure will be. It is not uncommon to use only one of these strategies to isolate the effects. The primary challenge with using only one isolation strategy is to gain credibility in the eyes of the client and governance bodies. Credibility is in the eyes of the beholder. If the client thinks that using only one isolation strategy will suffice and the evaluator agrees it's a sound approach, then go for it. It must be emphasized, however, that credibility increases as more of these building blocks are used.

Pre-/Post-Initiative Analysis

The essence of pre-/post-initiative analysis is to establish a baseline period before the change and then a second period, called the treatment period, after the change. The focusing question of this analysis is: What changes in the key performance variables occurred after deployment as compared to the base period? In order for this question to be answered, the base period and the evaluation period must be as similar to one another as possible. Other than the initiative, no major events or potential influences on the key performance variables should be different during the base or treatment periods. Otherwise, changes in performance during the treatment period could be attributed to these extraneous influences and not necessarily to the initiative.

As part of the analysis, all other potential influencing factors must be accounted for. The client, change practitioner, and others will have to determine whether these influencing factors had a similar impact on the key performance variables during both the base period and the treatment period. This can be a tall order. In part, this gets back to the discussion about the comprehensive nature of strategic change: There are just so many potential influencing factors. Some people faced with this kind of complexity might be tempted to just throw up their hands and surrender, but complexity can be tamed. Even if these other influences do exist and even if these influencing factors do impact the key performance variables, other isolation strategies can be employed to effectively deal with this situation.

What are some examples of these powerful influencing factors on the key performance variables? Seasonality of business performance is a common one. Retail businesses in the United States, for example, often gain more than half of their revenue during the last three months of the year. Sales cycles for specific retail stores also respond to regional or local cultural activities, sporting events, and the like. This is why retail businesses use same-store sales for a pre-/post-initiative measure. This involves comparing the sales of each individual store in one month (or quarter) with the sales of this same store in the same month (or quarter) of the previous year. This approach yields the truest picture of sales trends.

The overall performance of the economy is another powerful influence. Recessionary periods cannot be directly compared to nonrecessionary periods, unless certain adjustments are made. The likely impact of the change initiative would pale in comparison to the effects of strong recessionary influences. Recessionary periods may disproportionately affect certain industries or regional geographic areas. If so, these influences must be taken into account.

Several influencing factors occur internal to the organization as well. Restructuring and downsizing, for example, will influence people's performance, even if these people were not directly affected by these actions. Survivorship issues can linger with employees for months after the restructuring, introducing chronic performance problems.

There are some important considerations when planning a pre-/post-initiative analysis to isolate the effects of an initiative:

☐ Select a base period before deployment that is long enough to establish the appropriate quantity and quality of data.

☐ Identify potential influencing factors on performance other than those associated with the change initiative.

☐ Select a treatment period after the deployment that compares with the base period and accounts for extraneous factors and potential influences.

☐ Make sure that the data will be in a form that can be readily collected. If the data are not collected in a way that can be readily utilized in the evaluation, the evaluation plan must be revised to work with data that are available.

The pre-/post-initiative analysis is rarely used as a stand-alone strategy to isolate the effects of a strategic change initiative. This is true mostly because there are just too many other potential influencing factors from which to isolate. Often, the pre-/post-initiative analysis is used as a building block for other isolation strategies.

COMPARISON GROUPS

The essence of a comparison, or control, group is to establish two groups of participants that differ only in their experience with the change initiative. The focusing question that this strategy attempts to answer is: How did the key variables for the treatment group change in comparison to the other groups? In an experimental setting, comparison groups are fairly straightforward to set up. In a business setting, this can be more challenging. The approach to evaluation has to adapt to the needs of the organization, and not vice versa. It is unlikely that any organization would modify or delay the rollout of a strategically critical program to make the life of the evaluator easier. Evaluation must adapt to the realities of the business.

The good news is that by building evaluation activities into the design and development of the initiative, natural opportunities arise to better evaluate—and isolate—the effects of the initiative. The two most commonly used and most effective opportunities come through the use of pilots and sequencing.

Pilots. The essential purpose of a pilot is to try something out on a smaller, more manageable scale before attempting full-scale deployment. Bugs can be worked out. Operationally, pilots engage some people in the strategic initiative while leaving most people out. This allows natural comparison groups to be created. The performance of those who are involved in the initiative, the treatment group, can be compared to those who are not in the treatment group but who otherwise are similar to those in the treatment group.

For example, a manufacturing company wanted to evaluate the business impact of a Six Sigma initiative before it was expanded throughout the company. The manufacturing facility in which Six Sigma had been deployed for the past year was compared to a second facility that was similar in size and similar in other important characteristics. The key variable was the number of defects detected in the plant. The analysis showed that the Six Sigma plant had 18% fewer in-plant defects than the comparison plant. Although this result was sufficient for company management to proceed with continued (but not full) deployment of Six Sigma, it could be argued that additional analysis could be done to further isolate the effects. It's possible that other factors (e.g., increased teamwork, training, and reinvigorated supervision that accompanied Six Sigma) also could have contributed to the results. In these cases, further strategies to isolate the effects of Six Sigma would be called for. Chapter 6 explores how to maximize the value of pilots and isolate the effects of the initiative.

Sequencing. The comprehensive and large-scale nature of a strategic change initiative usually means that the deployment of this initiative is done in a series of phases. This phased approach might look like deployment on a division-by-division basis or perhaps deployment that follows a series of geographic regions. Similar to the situation with pilots, a situation is created whereby some people have been involved in the strategic initiative but some people have not. Once again, natural comparison groups are created that are comparable along certain key dimensions (e.g., geographic region, size of business operations, tenure and experience of the people, leadership capability, seasonality of the business). Having these dimensions similar for both treatment and comparison groups will remove these dimensions (or "nuisance variables" as statisticians call these) from the data analysis. Therefore, when isolating the effects of the change, the changes in performance will be largely attributed to the change and not to these other variables.

For example, a series of action learning workshops (or "gut check sessions" as these were called by the participants) were conducted for each of 23 business units for a financial services company. These workshops required the business unit leader to meet with a selected group of one-level-downs drawn from the other business units in a three-day workshop. The purpose of these workshops was for the business leader to present a vexing business problem and then engage this extended group of participants to find a solution. The team of OD facilitators began with two business units, and every two weeks would engage two more business units in this initiative.

After two months, the initiative was evaluated by comparing the first two business units with two comparable business units that had not yet gone through the initiative. Impressive gains were made by the first two (treatment) groups in their application of innovative problem-solving techniques as compared to the latter two (control) groups. Note in this example that the level of evaluation was set at level 3, application. Evaluation at level 4 (business impact) was not considered appropriate at this point in time, given the long timeframe that the results of these workshops would take to affect business results. Level 4 and 5 evaluations were conducted one year after the workshops were completed. This brings up a limitation of using the sequencing of deployment for the purposes of isolation: the production of monetary benefits often has an incubation time, whereby the monetary benefits produced by the change initiative can take a year or longer to materialize. Evaluating these benefits too early would yield a false-negative result.

Expert Estimation

Expert estimation is perhaps the most important and most widely used of all methods to isolate the effects of a change initiative. Experts include end users of the initiative products or services, supervisors and managers of the end users, functional experts who worked on developing or deploying the initiative, vendors, contractors, consultants, and customers. These experts are asked to report and reflect on their experiences and observations to offer their estimation of the effect of the initiative on the organization. Gaining the input of many of these experts from many perspectives provides a robust and diverse picture of how the initiative affected the organization. Credibility for this approach grows as more voices join the chorus of estimation.

Expert estimation is adaptable and can be used to isolate the effects when no other isolation strategy is possible or feasible. For example, a government agency director wanted to know the impact of a leadership development initiative on schedule attainment and mission success. Because every mission was unique and the scheduling of activities varied widely, the complexity of this situation posed too great a challenge for pre-/post-initiative or comparison group analyses. That left expert estimation as the only strategy for isolating the benefits of this initiative. The evaluation plan called for conducting two telephone-based interviews of leadership development participants and others who were involved in achieving the missions. Interview questions explored enhanced productivity and faster schedule completion. Respondents provided data that isolated the effects of leadership development on these two performance variables.

Utilizing expert estimation to isolate the effects of a change initiative follows these four steps:

1. *Understand what effects must be isolated.* There must be a clear understanding of the performance variables. In the government agency example, these variables were productivity and schedule attainment. Operational definitions were prepared so that people will knew how their actions were measured. Productivity was operationally defined as the hours saved per week as a result of the leadership development initiative. Schedule completion was operationally defined as the number of hours saved by all mission personnel resulting from the mission being accomplished earlier than scheduled. These changes came as a direct result of leadership development.

2. *Write the isolation questions.* The operational definitions shed light on how to ask people to estimate the impact of a change initiative. These questions should follow a logical and intuitive sequence and be written in a way that is understandable to the estimators. For example, building off the previous operational definition of productivity, questions could pertain to how many hours per week the respondent saved, multiply these hours by standard values of money and time, ask for a percentage estimate of how much of these benefits resulted from leadership development (contribution factor), and conclude by asking on a percentage basis how confident the respondent was in his or her estimation (error factor). Chapter 9 delves into the specifics of how to best use surveys to isolate the effects of an initiative.

3. *Identify a group of estimators.* With estimation, the more the merrier—up to a point. Estimation is strengthened when a diverse set of experts is used. Customers and vendors in particular are viewed as extremely credible sources for the impact of the initiative; however, they will likely have little understanding of the initiative itself. End users of the initiative (e.g., those who participated in a leadership development workshop) can speak

forcefully from their own experience, but they often do not see the big picture. Sponsors of the initiative will see the big picture and the overall context for the initiative, but they will have limited personal experience of the initiative. Everyone holds a piece of the truth. A diverse set of estimators will produce the most accurate portrayal of the truth.

4. *Decide on methodology and timing.* The three choices boil down to interviews, surveys, and focus groups. Often, all of these methods are used together to estimate the value of an initiative. The case study in Chapter 11 provides an example of how interviews and surveys were used to determine the ROI of executive coaching. Interviews provide the highest-quality data because of the close interaction between the evaluator and the respondent. Interviewing is time intensive and can increase the cost of an evaluation. Surveys are efficient, although in dealing with more complex isolation requirements, they may not offer high-quality data. Basically, respondents may get confused while attempting to complete portions of the survey and, having no one to immediately turn to with questions or issues, may simply give up and not provide complete data. Focus groups try to finesse the higher quality of data gained with interviews with the greater efficiency of surveys. Several experts, often eight to twelve, can be assembled in a focus group that is facilitated by the evaluator. Respondents can talk amongst themselves about their experiences and ask the evaluator any questions they might have. The evaluator facilitates the group to answer the series of questions and can continue probing until he or she is satisfied that the data are complete and of a sufficient quality level.

How do all three of these approaches work together? Let's look at a case study that developed a plan to isolate the effects of implementing a new relationship management sales process.

CASE STUDY: ISOLATING THE EFFECTS OF AN INITIATIVE

A manufacturing organization had recently implemented a new sales process with its dealerships. This new process emphasized relationship selling rather than the commodity product approach to selling that the company had used for decades. This meant that the sales force was now expected to understand the deeper value needs of its customers, build a relationship with them, and engage customers to consider a comprehensive set of product and service offerings to meet their needs. This new approach to customers was intended to replace the previous way of dealing with customers characterized by presenting a range of products to the customer and then rapidly discounting the price of the products to gain customer interest in a desperate attempt to sell the product to the customer.

This new approach was expected to generate extra sales; in fact, it was expected to increase sales by 40% within the first fiscal year. There were no changes to the product line. With the end of the fiscal year approaching, the business leadership wanted to know how to evaluate the impact of the new sales process.

The recommended approach to evaluation was threefold:

1. *Compare pre-/post-initiative data.* Annual sales for the year before the new sales process was implemented would be compared with the annual sales of the year operating under the new sales process. The new sales process was implemented in the first quarter of the year. This meant that for the post-initiative period, less than one year's worth of sales under the new process (i.e., three quarters worth) would be compared with a pre-initiative period consisting of an entire year's worth of sales. This approach, while unbalanced, was viewed as being extra conservative by placing a higher hurdle rate for the initiative to show increased sales. Besides, data were only available from all dealers on an annual basis. It would have been too onerous and costly to break out the sales data in smaller quarterly chunks.

2. *Natural comparison groups were created.* Not every dealership participated in the new sales process implementation. This opened possibilities for comparison groups to be created. A comparison was proposed to match a dealership that did not participate with another dealership that did participate in the new process. These two dealerships or cohorts were similar enough along key dimensions to satisfy the client and the evaluator that these two dealerships were comparable. These dimensions included product mix, size, experience of the salespeople, and economic conditions. Several cohorts or pairings of dealerships were made. Sales differences, or deltas, between the paired dealerships were noted and accumulated. Combined, these data presented a powerful case to show the effect of the change initiative on sales performance.

3. *Expert estimations were made by key groups.* Salespeople, sales managers, and a select group of customers were interviewed to

assess the impact of the new sales approach on increasing sales. Each group estimated the impact that the new process had on sales and expressed the confidence they had in their estimates on a percentage basis.

This case study emphasizes the point that every evaluation requires judgment and making trade-offs. For example, judgments are made about how the cohorts are defined and selected and who would be included in the expert estimation process. The evaluator and the client together made these important decisions. The evaluator ensures that rigorous measurement methodology is employed, while the client adds a dose of reality. Some key issues emerged with using isolation strategies for the new sales process:

☐ *Dealing with many variables.* This analysis was awash in variables: the varied abilities of the sales managers, the ranges of salespersons' tenure and their varying degrees of product knowledge, and the incentive programs that varied by dealership were just a few. How can the evaluation deal with these variables? There are two major ways. The first is to ensure that the treatment groups and the comparison groups have similar characteristics along these lines. Next, and if this first method cannot be done, the end user and expert estimations can include these variables in the estimation process. In other words, the evaluator would ask people to estimate the contribution that the quality of sales management made to their performance or perhaps the incentive plans. These estimations would be done in conjunction with estimations of the effect of the initiative.

☐ *Use of multiple measures.* In this example, three isolation strategies were used. Although this approach will likely increase the credibility of the evaluation, it also increases the complexity. All data have to be weaved together to create a credible picture. Any inconsistencies have to be ironed out before the evaluation can be completed. Apparent interaction effects must be explored. This can require additional evaluation activities. For example, what if some dealerships showed that the incentive plan they used was the primary contributor of business value, even more so than the initiative? These incentive plans would have to be further explored and documented and some reasonable explanation given for this effect.

☐ *Sample size.* Comparing only one dealership that participated in the initiative to just one dealership that did not participate could be viewed as too small a sample size to produce meaningful data. Therefore, many dealership cohorts were selected. Where do you draw the line? Just how big does the sample size have to be? Larger samples are more valid or representative of the larger population from which the samples were drawn; however, larger samples drive up the cost of the evaluation.

We are, after all, trying to isolate the effects of an initiative, not win the Nobel prize. There are statistical guidelines for drawing samples. Briefly, samples should be drawn randomly, and these samples should be randomly assigned to treatments. At the risk of incurring the wrath of statisticians, these guidelines are often not completely practical in real-world settings. How many business leaders, for example, would allow the evaluator to decide which dealerships will be included in the sales training and which dealerships would be left out? Not many to be sure. The bottom line is that both the evaluator and the client make commonsense judgments about the size and shape of the samples to be evaluated.

Focus of Evaluation: Judgment, not Numbers

Evaluation is about judgment. It is a formal process of creating knowledge and of making choices about what knowledge to gain. These choices are made in the context of the organization and the external environment. There is inevitably a tremendous amount of complexity to be dealt with. Realistically, trade-offs must be made and business realities must be contended with. These judgments are the realm of strategic change valuation.

It is important not to get caught up in the numbers. Measurement creates numbers. Evaluation creates knowledge. Valuation assembles this knowledge to determine the total value or worth of a strategic change initiative.

CHAPTER 6

Deploy the Strategic Change Initiative and Evaluate Progress

Deploying a strategic change initiative without the evaluation component is like sending a sports team out onto the field of play blindfolded. The players may pick up on some cues—the cheering of the fans, the sounds made by the other players—but the quality of their play will be diminished by the lack of visual information. The point here is that evaluation provides more than just the score; it provides information that enables greater performance, and greater performance during deployment translates into a bigger impact on the bottom line.

Bottom-line OD makes three significant contributions to successfully deploying change initiatives:

1. Fully integrates evaluation into change management
2. Builds mastery in the mechanics of evaluation
3. Maximizes the value of pilots

This chapter explores each of these three areas in detail.

VALUE-BASED DEPLOYMENT: INTEGRATING EVALUATION AND CHANGE

Value-based deployment integrates evaluation into the deployment process (Figure 6.1). This approach opens up new possibilities for:

☐ Sustaining sponsorship of the initiative
☐ Engaging team members for effective deployment

Figure 6.1 Value-based deployment.

☐ Making midcourse corrections to increase the value of the initiative

Sustaining Sponsorship of the Initiative

Strong sponsorship of a change initiative is not a right: It is something that must be earned every day. Earning the continued support of the sponsor depends in part on how effectively the sponsor believes the initiative is delivering the expected value. It is therefore critical to regularly share with the sponsor how the deployment of the initiative is on track to deliver the goods.

Today's business environment is dynamic. There are many investment proposals competing for limited resources. A sponsor who has given the green light to deploy an initiative already has invested a fair amount of resources into the effort; however, the dynamic nature of the business environment means that things change. Change practitioners cannot assume that the green light to deploy will ensure smooth sailing for the rest of the initiative. Business priorities may shift. Sponsors may lose focus or clarity about how the change initiative will positively affect top business goals. Sponsors who ask "what have you done for me lately" are possibly showing symptoms of this loss of focus or clarity. They are not likely to sustain their support for the initiative for much longer.

There may be legitimate reasons why a change initiative has to be cut back in scope or even stopped. Many times, however, change initiatives are cut back because the change practitioner failed to continue to tell the story about how the change initiative will achieve business goals.

The result is waning sponsorship. What are the telltale signs that sustained sponsorship may be in jeopardy (Figure 6.2)?

1. *Sponsors talk but don't walk support.* Saying the right words is important, but if the client's deeds do not follow pronouncements of support for the change effort, then the client's sustained support for the initiative is on thin ice. Sponsorship is more than intention, it is taking action. These actions must be visible and be taken consistently throughout the change initiative. Words and deeds must match. What are some examples of sponsorship misdeeds? The client becomes unavailable to participate in important initiative meetings. She appoints a subordinate to handle key initiative roles that she had previously taken on. She delays or defers decision making critical for the initiative. Plus, all of these actions are taken while still professing support for the initiative.

2. *Sponsors don't even talk support as they have in the past.* At this point sponsorship is hanging by a thread. Not only is the client not taking action, but statements of support become few and far between. What does this look like? Clients nor their representa-

Figure 6.2 Telltale signs that sponsorship is wavering.

tives regularly attend important initiative meetings. The initiative is no longer a standing agenda item on the client's regular leadership team meetings. Speeches, company news articles, and other communication opportunities are not utilized for the initiative.

3. *Sponsors begin to walk away with their support.* The final stage of disengagement is when the client begins to withdraw support for the initiative. Investments and resources are diverted to other projects. Pilots or other deployment timelines are pushed back, often with little notice or explanation. New initiatives, and perhaps even competing initiatives, are funded at the apparent expense of continuing to fund the initiative budget.

RESPONDING TO THESE TELLTALE SIGNS: SUSTAINING THE SPONSORSHIP

What do you do if you begin to spot these symptoms? And how does bottom-line OD better position the change practitioner to effectively deal with the underlying issues? In the previous chapters business goals were explicitly linked to initiative objectives. Evaluation objectives were based on the initiative objectives. This critical line-of-sight linkage can be leveraged to sustain sponsorship.

☐ *Provide regular status updates.* An important part of having the sponsor stay the course is to provide regular updates on how well the evaluation objectives are being met. It is also critical to share with the sponsor the implications of the evaluation and discuss any action steps that the sponsor (or others) may need to take. Also, leverage the relationships that exist with key influential players. The sponsor will look to these key players when making decisions that may impact the initiative. Provide regular updates to the key players, and continue to emphasize how the initiative will help them achieve their personal and organization goals.

☐ *Ask the sponsor for help.* Sponsors need to feel that they have "skin in the game." Asking the sponsor to help with a problem situation deepens their engagement and sense of personal commitment. Sponsors then can be seen as leaders in the field of battle as they stake their personal prestige on the initiative success.

☐ *Focus key communication messages on the business value of the initiative.* Reinforce these messages in different media and over time. Don't assume that people will read, retain, and remember every communication. Highlight messages with success stories drawn from the experiences that people have had with the initiative. Communicate in a variety of ways about how the initiative has created value for people and for the business.

☐ *Leverage the governance team as the central decision-making body.* Decentralizing sponsorship for the initiative spreads out the ownership for making the initiative a success. Leverage this ownership to sustain and grow the momentum for change. Several actions can be taken to accomplish this goal:

1. *Post and review weekly updates on project progress.* Everyone involved in the change coalition should be kept apprised of the project status in order to keep the progress on task, reward achievement, and correct missteps. Weekly updates should be disseminated to all change coalition team members so that everyone is apprised of critical initiative information. This information can include upcoming milestones, significant due dates, deployment status, stories of people who have gone above and beyond the call of duty, and so on. This information helps the governance team keep in touch with the initiative.

2. *Surface and resolve challenges to the deployment.* Every deployment has its hiccups. It is important to spot these issues right away and bring them to the attention of the governance team for resolution as appropriate. These issues are better resolved as they occur rather than after they have been allowed to linger or fester. Governance team meetings can have a standard agenda item to surface and resolve these issues so that the deployment can move forward with minimal disruption.

3. *Leverage active, visible support of governance team members for the project.* Sponsorship is a performing art. Governance team members must occasionally be seen at the front lines providing support and boosting morale. These leaders can lend their personal prestige to the initiative by showing people what they do to support the initiative. Leaders can participate in pilots or workshops or other activities to show their support.

4. *Form measurement subteams to accelerate data collection and analysis.* The governance team will appreciate a steady diet of initiative performance metrics. Establishing a subteam to do this will ensure consistency and quality in data collection and reporting.

5. *Form a communications subteam to drive effective communications.* The creation of a subteam assigned to the specific task

of facilitating communication within the initiative and between the initiative and outside groups helps ensure that communication does not falter throughout the remainder of the initiative. This team can work with the governance team members to craft specific messages and communications.

Engaging Team Members for Effective Deployment

People like to create things and generally enjoy challenging situations where their creativity is needed. Beginning an initiative is usually accompanied with people feeling energized and excited about what is ahead. Strategic change initiatives are prolonged, complex, and at times frustrating. People's energy reserves are constantly being depleted. This is perhaps especially true during deployment. The creativity of the design and development phases has given way to the harsh reality of hand-to-hand combat: conducting workshops, coaching people, and confronting resisters.

This energy must be renewed and people revitalized if their active engagement is to be sustained. Fortunately, people's energy is a renewable resource, and bottom-line OD opens options for change practitioners to sustain the engagement of team members.

REINFORCE ACCOUNTABILITY WITH MEANINGFUL PERFORMANCE FEEDBACK

People generally want to make a significant difference. They want to feel valued and recognized for their contributions. Accountability and feedback are essential in order to recognize people for their efforts. How does this work? First, make change team members accountable to achieve specific evaluation objectives. Next, ensure that people have the support they need to achieve these objectives. Position project milestones as opportunities to check in on their progress in achieving these milestones. In order for this process to be effective, leaders, managers, and change practitioners must come from a place of helping, not judging. Performance issues will inevitably come up. This underscores the importance of mutually engaging in problem solving to address these performance issues.

PROVIDE RECOGNITION AND CREATE HEROES

No deployment runs totally smoothly. There is always the unexpected. Strategic change is highly complex, so the change team members will have to respond nimbly to the inevitable issues that crop up. Change teams operate most effectively when each team member can make on-the-spot decisions to keep the deployment rolling. This requires initiative from team members. Recognize those team members who step up and take on these unexpected issues to successfully move the initiative along. Document their exploits, and create heroes who show by example how others may also successfully deal with the unexpected. Be sure to utilize communication mechanisms for recognition, such as company newsletters, department meetings, and so on. Think about creating awards. For example, a change team that established a corporate university called The Academy distributed "academy award" statuettes for performance above and beyond the call of duty in creating this new learning capability for the company. A Hollywood-style celebration was held to announce the winners and hand out the awards.

Making Midcourse Corrections to Increase the Value of the Initiative

Bottom-line evaluation activities generate knowledge. Acting on this knowledge creates value. Taking these actions during deployment increases the ultimate value of the initiative. Signposts are established to trigger these actions, and when linked to milestones, they can trigger significant actions at critical times during the deployment.

A signpost is a point in time when evaluation data are reviewed. These review points are most effective when they are tied to project milestones. For example, a project milestone may be the "completion of sales management workshops for the eastern region of a company." A signpost is established at this point: the percentage of managers who achieve a score of at least 85% on the postworkshop learning comprehension test. If a review of the actual score shows a comprehension level of only 55%, then red flags must be raised. These managers cannot apply what they have not learned, so corrective actions are clearly warranted. Actions will be taken to increase the managers' comprehension level. For example, online refresher courses could be offered for those whose scores fell below the 85% threshold.

Once the signpost has been read and the corrective actions are decided on, it is important to take these corrective actions immediately. Work with the appropriate leaders to understand the performance issue, walk them through the implications of the issue, and mutually explore corrective actions. This exploration needs to be undertaken with a minimum amount of defensiveness. Block blame. Gain an understanding of what caused the performance issue so that it can be corrected in an effective and timely way. Recognize that many people contributed to the issue and that many people will be required to address the issue. Focus on the solution, not who contributed to the problem.

Fix the problem at the appropriate level. Senior leaders who have empowered initiative leaders and others to fix problems do not need to get involved in the nuances of fixing the problems. Inform senior leaders that the problem has been fixed. Bring them the good news, bad news story: the good news is that we fixed the problem, the bad news was that the problem threatened to delay the deployment. Concentrate on educating leaders about how to prevent these problems from ocurring again. Only involve senior leaders when the performance issue cannot be fixed without their involvement.

Don't assume that the corrective actions were successful. Conduct the assessment again and check to make sure that the actions were effective. Be sure to share with the extended change team what the problem was and how it was fixed. Treat this episode as a best practice and part of building up the knowledge base of effective change management. This provides another opportunity to recognize people's efforts to fix a serious problem. More folklore of hero worship presents itself. The key message here is not to expect a problem-free deployment, but rather to expect that people successfully deal with the problems that will inevitably occur.

MASTERING THE MECHANICS OF EVALUATION

Data collection has to rank as one of people's least favorite activities. It is a mechanical exercise, but if the nuts and bolts of the strategic change initiative are not tightly secured, the entire strategic structure can collapse. Effectively collecting and organizing data are essential in order for the evaluation to be successful. Data collection during deployment also offers an early glimpse into the ultimate success of the initiative. Exit polling of participants reveals their initial reactions to the change initiative, what they are learning, and how well they are applying what they have learned. These data have big implications for how the initiative will ultimately produce business results.

Collecting and Organizing Data

The master guide for data collection is the evaluation plan. This plan contains the key variables that must be tracked. In this way, the data collection is an extension of the line-of-sight connection to the top business goal. As illustrated in Figure 6.3, the business goal, initiative objec-

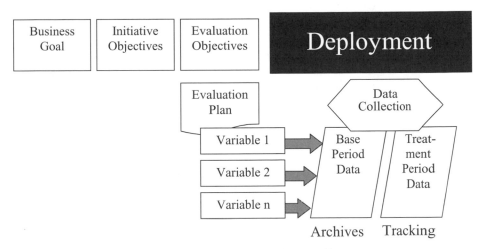

Figure 6.3 Line-of-sight data collection.

tive, and evaluation objectives are inextricably linked. The evaluation plan, which contains the key variables, is an extension of the evaluation objectives. Data collection focuses on those key variables in two distinct phases: the base period and the treatment period.

The base period represents a time before the change initiative was deployed. This time period represents a steady state for the key variables. In today's business environment there is really no such thing as a steady state, but the base period comes as close as possible, given business conditions. Seasonality is an example of a business condition. Sales of snowblowers in Iowa occur mostly in the fall and early winter. If a key variable for an evaluation was the sale of these items, then similar calendar months would have to be compared to each other. A base period of July could not be compared to a treatment period of November. Simply too much of the variation in sales would be a result of the change in seasons, not the sales management initiative.

The treatment period represents a time during or after which the initiative was deployed. Comparisons of the key variables during the treatment period are compared with those of the base period. Changes in the variables may be attributed to the impact of the initiative. We say may here because the effects of the initiative have not been isolated. These pre-/post-initiative comparisons are the first big building block for isolating the effects. Please refer to Chapter 5 for a more detailed explanation of isolating the effects.

Base data are collected through archives, while treatment data are gathered through real-time tracking. Both of these data-gathering methods are coordinated so that apples-to-apples comparisons are made. For example, if base data archives only have the number of units of snowblowers sold and not revenue data, then the data tracking during the treatment period will have to collect the same kind of data. If data collected during the treatment period was based on sales revenue, then these data could not be directly compared to the unit data.

It is also a good idea to begin developing standard data display charts. Display the data with these charts as the data are collected. This ensures that direct data comparisons can be made and gets people more comfortable with how the data will be displayed. Many external factors may influence the business and by implication the key variables. It is important to record these external events and the time in which these occurred. Later, when the data are analyzed, any peaks or valleys in the data may be at least partially explained by these external factors. This effect also comes up again when isolating the effects of the initiative on the key variables. Other influences must be noted and factored in to the analysis.

Conduct Impact Studies During Deployment

Often, there is great anticipation for the early returns of data collected during the initial stages of deployment. Impact studies can be conducted that will shed light on:

- ☐ The initial reaction of the participants to the change (level 1)
- ☐ The degree to which people effectively know what they must do differently (level 2)
- ☐ How well people are applying their new skills and knowledge to accomplish the change initiative objectives (level 3)

These impact studies form the basis to make any midcourse corrections on the deployment. These studies, in order to be effective, should include a description of how data were collected, samples of data collection tools, analysis of the data according to the key variables, conclusions drawn from the data, and recommendations for the deployment. These recommendations point the way to any midcourse corrections that must be made, which underscores the need for these impact studies to be produced in a timely way. Recommendations to improve the deployment of the initiative have little value when these come too late to be acted upon. In addition to the quantitative data, qualitative data can also be collected at this time. Interviews with key people can capture important insights that might be lost if the attempt to collect these data happened after the deployment. These interviews can produce stories of how people deployed and worked with the initiative to make it successful. These stories not only contain nuggets of insights about the change but also can pack an emotional wallop that numbers alone cannot readily convey.

Maximizing the Value of Pilots

The success of any show is created during the rehearsals. Rehearsals enable the show's producers to test the stagecraft, coach the actors throughout their performance, and reinforce everyone's responsibilities to make the show come off without a hitch. In order to be effective, rehearsals must closely resemble the conditions of an actual performance. Managing a pilot before full deployment of a change initiative is no different. Pilots are most effective when conducted on location, representing the diversity of the organization's population and enacting all facets of the change initiative.

Pilots represent deployment on a smaller, more manageable scale. This approach allows change practitioners to find out what does and does not work and readily fix the problems. Fixing these problems on a smaller scale can be done more quickly and effectively than if these problems had to be corrected during the full deployment of the initiative. Pilots also can create anticipation and excitement for full deployment. This is likely the first opportunity people will have to see what the new changes will look like. People involved in the pilot can feel special, knowing that they are the first to experience the change and that they have a great opportunity to influence how the change will be managed for the entire organization.

There are six important ways to maximize the value of pilots. Given the level of investment that the pilot represents, it is important to gain as much as possible from the pilot experience.

1. *Ensure that the pilot population reflects the greater organization.* Selecting a location or locations for the pilot is an extremely important decision. The primary criterion for this selection process is ensuring that the pilot reflects the diversity of the organization. Cost of the pilot, while important to consider, is secondary. The diversity of the organization here refers to cultures, languages, size of the population or facility, business performance, leadership styles, degree of unionization, and other factors that are considered distinguishing characteristics. Identifying these

characteristics is based on the belief that these characteristics may influence the outcome of the deployment. If, for example, the leaders believe that deploying a new performance management process will be more challenging in larger, unionized facilities in North America, then this kind of facility would be a strong candidate for the pilot.

2. *Conduct usability testing.* In recent years, more change practitioners are employing usability testing. Usability testing is in a sense a pilot within a pilot. This testing involves exposing small numbers of people to certain aspects of the deployment materials and processes. The reactions of the participants are closely monitored, and their feedback is immediately incorporated into the deployment materials. For example, a job aid created for supervisors to conduct the new performance management discussions can be examined through usability testing. This job aid would be reviewed with a small number of supervisors—say, four or five— and their immediate reactions would be recorded. Sometimes this recording can be done via video or audio media for later review. A role-play can be performed to see how the supervisors use the job aid. Issues or questions that arise can be fed back to the developers of the job aid, and they in turn can make the improvements in a timely fashion. In some cases, a room with one-way glass is used, much like a consumer focus group, which enables the developers of the material to directly observe how people are using their materials and to make any needed corrections in real time.

3. *Take the opportunity to forecast benefits.* Pilots offer a golden opportunity to gauge actual utilization and application of the change process to a work environment. These data can be readily analyzed to forecast application on a broader scale. If a forecast was done during the design phase, then the pilot offers an opportunity to check the assumptions that were made to support the forecast. Making adjustments to the forecasts will mean making new predictions about the value that the initiative will likely add to the business. Even if a forecast was not made earlier in the initiative, a forecast based on pilot data can be valuable. Pilot data are real, albeit on a smaller scale. ROI forecasts based on pilot data can be accurate. Chapter 8 discusses forecasting in more detail.

4. *Examine roles and responsibilities.* It is important to know not just what the pilots accomplished but how well these accom-

plishments were achieved. The pilot offers the opportunity to "clear the decks for action" and make sure that all players know their role in the deployment and are clear on their responsibilities to make it successful. Gaps or redundancies in these roles and responsibilities can be uncovered and dealt with appropriately. For example, if after completing a performance management workshop the supervisors still struggle with applying the material to their work environment, a new deployment role may need to be added to address this shortfall. A new role of performance coach could be established to work with selected supervisors to ensure that they effectively apply the material.

5. *Establish effective lines of communication.* Pilots operate in accelerated time. The initiative team will need to be nimble in how the pilots are conducted, knowledge is accumulated, and decisions are made. These decisions will likely require input or approval from organization leaders, including the client or initiative sponsor. In any event, these leaders will be keenly interested in how the pilots are proceeding. Normal lines of communication often prove inadequate to match the speed of the pilot. New lines of communication must be established to ensure that decisions are made in a timely way and potential barriers are quickly removed. A plant manager, for example, who at the last minute becomes reluctant to allow his managers to participate in the pilot will need to have a discussion with his boss. This discussion will have to happen quickly if the pilot is to remain on schedule. Establishing a rapid-response process ensures that people's priorities get straightened out if need be.

6. *Conduct a debriefing immediately after the pilot has been completed.* The pilot generates a wealth of data. The more this wealth of data is mined, the greater the opportunity for learning important lessons from the pilot. Given the accelerated timeframe in which pilots typically operate, there is little time or enthusiasm for writing detailed reports on the success of the pilot. Moreover, full deployment usually follows closely on the heels of the pilot, so there is little time to even write and distribute these reports. Conducting formal debriefings is an effective way to gain the needed lessons in a timely way. These debriefings are formal in the sense that they are not just open discussion periods but are organized around answering specific questions. Examples of questions include the following:

☐ How well did the performance coaching process work?

☐ Did the performance management process translate well to other cultures?

☐ How can the performance management job aid be better utilized by the supervisors?

☐ How well did the change management workshops prepare leaders for the deployment?

Discussing these questions fosters greater learning about the pilots, provides a forum for best practices to be shared, and effectively builds a team that is ready to tackle the challenges of full deployment.

CHAPTER 7

Reflect on the Business Impact Utilizing Post-Initiative Evaluations

The evaluation activities conducted during the deployment of the strategic change initiative have produced a wealth of data. The challenge now is to separate the wheat from the chaff. Data are analyzed to yield the essential information required to understand the organizational impact of the initiative. Organization leaders then reflect on this information to make decisions about how best to develop their organization. This process of analysis and reflection is accomplished with the following steps:

1. Separating hard from soft data
2. Converting benefits to monetary value
3. Qualifying the monetary benefits
4. Tabulating the costs of the initiative
5. Calculating return on investment
6. Leveraging strategic insights

Each of these steps is discussed in detail in this chapter.

SEPARATING HARD FROM SOFT DATA

Analysis Requires Both Hard and Soft Data

All data are meaningful. Just because data are considered soft—subjective and difficult to measure—does not mean that they have no place in the evaluation. Strategic change practitioners have mostly relied on soft data to convey the value of their initiatives to clients and business leaders. No leader would say that improved decision making, increased employee loyalty, or more satisfied customers were not important outcomes of change initiatives. Clearly, articulating these benefits is necessary, but not sufficient to understand and increase the value of strategic change initiatives. Leaders today want and deserve more—they want to also know the bottom-line impact of the initiative. Providing this knowledge takes us out of soft data and into the realm of hard data.

Understanding the bottom-line impact requires us to look more closely at the hard data. Hard data are objective, easier to measure, and more straightforward to convert to monetary value. Business mostly runs on hard data, and therefore these data have a great deal of credibility with business leaders. A change initiative that positively impacts project completion times, employee productivity, and order shipment fidelity in addition to the soft benefits will gain great credibility with business leaders. The point here is that evaluating a strategic change initiative requires both kinds of data—hard and soft. Bottom-line OD focuses on hard data partly because these data have been underutilized in the evaluation of strategic change initiatives.

Overcoming Concerns of Using Hard Data

Why have hard data been underutilized? Strategic change practitioners have voiced two major concerns about using hard data to evaluate their work. One concern was that it was not possible to measure what was truly important for the organization, given that the greatest value of the strategic change was intangible. Although this concern is valid in many cases, this does not preclude evaluating hard data. In fact, evaluating hard and soft data go hand in hand. Improved project completion (hard) may have been possible only with improved decision making (soft); improved employee productivity (hard) may be an expression of loyalty (soft); and order shipment fidelity (hard) may be an important factor in creating more satisfied customers (soft). Both hard and soft data are important, and more to the point, both are of great interest to the initiative sponsors, clients, and organization leaders.

The second concern was that it was not possible to isolate the effects of a strategic change initiative. This assertion is hasty and shortchanges leaders, change practitioners, and others who are interested in knowing the value they create. We live in an imperfect world. There are no absolutes. Is it always possible to determine with great precision the impact that an initiative had on the organization—to isolate these effects from all of the other potential influences on the organization? No, it is not always possible, but this does not mean that we don't do the best we can with what we've got. We estimate and we put error limits on our estimations. We are conservative at every step in the process. We use multiple measures whenever possible. We look for creative ways to use comparison groups. We ask experts and participants their perspectives and viewpoints on the change process. We do many things to produce the most accurate and credible portrayal of the impact of an initiative on the organization.

Bottom-line OD is rigorous and utilizes proven measurement methodology. It is intended to add value for organization leaders and change practitioners. It is not an academic exercise. Business is based on estimations, assumptions, judgments, and—truth be known—guesswork. The point here is that bottom-line OD operates in a business environment, follows the same standards, and uses the same financial tools. This approach is not perfect to be sure, but it places the change practitioner on the same playing field, playing by the same rules as other businesspeople, which is a good thing.

Example of Using Hard and Soft Data

The leader of a large business unit within a global company wanted to know how successful an executive development pilot had been in improving executive performance. The company had just completed a major acquisition that by many accounts had not gone particularly well. Executives appeared demoralized by their experience. Depending on how successful this pilot had been, the initiative would be deployed for executives throughout the organization.

The business unit leader viewed increasing executive morale as a top priority, but she also faced other urgent business needs that required investments. It was decided that both hard and soft data were to be examined. Hard data were converted to monetary value. The leader

Table 7.1 Example of Hard and Soft Data Analysis

Unit of Measure—Hard Data	Monetary Value Standards	Convert to Monetary Value
Output measure: Productivity of participants	Hours saved per week. One hour = $75 40 hours per week 48 weeks in a year	Each executive reported hours saved per week Hours multiplied by standards Value accumulated for all coaching participants

Unit of Measure—Soft Data	Source of Data	Determining Benefits
Attitudes: Increasing morale after a bruising acquisition	Custom executive survey administered to participants and a cohort of executives Survey included a mix of direct and indirect items	Scores calculated for participants and cohorts Statistics (t-test) used to determine significance

expected this executive initiative to carry its own weight, that the financial benefits would at least cover the investments. Regardless of the ROI, however, if this initiative did not significantly improve morale, it would not be expanded to other areas in the organization.

Table 7.1 illustrates the process used for analyzing the data for both hard and soft measures. Executive productivity, an example of hard data, was determined by multiplying the number of hours an executive saved each week by the standard values. So, for example, an executive who saved 5 hours per week would produce (unqualified) benefits of

$$5 \text{ hours} \times \$75 \times 48 \text{ weeks} = \$18,000$$

These benefits were qualified by multiplying the dollar amount by the contribution (isolation) factor and the confidence (error) factor according to a process that is discussed in detail later in this chapter. Suffice it to say at this point that the qualified (or isolated) benefits for all participants were determined and then summed. Results showed that the initiative produced more than two dollars for every dollar invested, thus the initiative more than paid for itself.

With the investment issue successfully hurdled, how well did the initiative improve morale? A custom survey instrument was developed that used both direct and indirect questions to assess morale. Because other factors may have influenced morale, a cohort group was identified as a comparison to the group of initiative participants. A statistical analysis showed that the improvement in morale was not significant. Based on these findings, the business unit leader decided not to expand the executive development initiative. In this example, the hard data (productivity) did not carry as much weight as the soft data (morale), but both kinds of data were considered in making the final decision.

Converting Benefits to Monetary Value

This case study example also illustrates one way that benefits were converted to monetary value. There are three steps to this process:

1. Defining the unit of measure
2. Determining the standard values
3. Calculating the annualized benefits

Defining the Unit of Measure

In the case study, productivity was operationally defined as the "number of hours saved per week." This is called a *unit of measure*. There are four main categories for units of measure: output, time, cost, and quality. Output data deal with units produced, processed, inventoried, distributed, sold, or serviced. Time measures include project completion time, product development cycle time, production changeover delays, order response times, work-processing times, and many other time-related measures. Cost measures include unit costs, fixed costs (usually expressed as sales, general and administrative, or SG&A costs), variable costs (such as contractor fees), operating costs, and other measures. Quality measures include warranty costs, defects, rejects, scrap rates, customer transactions completed on first call, call routing accuracy, and a variety of other measures.

Selecting the most appropriate units of measure is done by the evaluator and the client or initiative sponsor. The evaluation objectives will typically point to one or more units of measure. An evaluation objective that specifies, for example, an increase in unit sales, clearly points to a unit of measurement such as "sales margin dollars for the 600-B product line." For the most part, the selection process is completed before deployment. The sooner these units of measure are selected, the better for the evaluation. The quality of pilot data will improve, data collection procedures can be put in place earlier, and real-time changes in the data can be tracked. Tracking sales margins for 600-B product salespeople over the course of a one-year sales process improvement initiative could produce many critical insights into how to improve the initiative, let alone how to increase sales volume.

In the current case study example, the evaluation was conducted after the executive development initiative had been completed, which limited the selection of the units of measure. As we have seen, integrating evaluation throughout the design, development, and deployment of the initiative opens options for understanding the impact of the initiative. This is also true with selecting units of measure. Given that understanding organizational impact is largely viewed through the lens of the units of measure, selecting these units is important. So, for example, if the business unit leader had called the evaluator earlier in the life cycle of the initiative, other units of measure might have presented themselves, such as "number of hours saved by peers through improved collaboration" or "number of hours saved by subordinates through improved leadership skills." Assessing these latter two units of measure would be difficult after the fact.

Determining Standard Values

Standard values are determined so that the unit of measure can be converted to monetary benefits. These values are standardized so that the calculations are consistent. It is critical to ensure apples-to-apples comparisons. For example, the standard value of $75 per hour for an executive's time will be used to calculate both productivity and cost. The cost of the program includes the executive's time spent participating in the initiative. The total number of hours spent by all participating executives was multiplied by $75. This calculation produces the total opportunity cost, or what the company effectively spent on the initiative in terms of executives' time. Having standard values ensures consistency in how data are calculated. For the most part, these standard values have already been determined by the organization. Typically, the human resources function maintains these values. If these values have not been determined by the organization, the evaluator will have to work with the appropriate people in the organization to determine the standard values.

Calculating Annualized Benefits

Annualized benefits are always used in ROI calculations. One-time benefits are excluded. Generally, only one year's worth of annualized benefits are included in the ROI calculation. Strategic change initiatives will likely produce benefits well beyond one year, but only using the first year of benefits is the conservative and most credible way to go.

The current case study illustrated how annualized monetary benefits were calculated. First, each executive who participated in the program reported the hours he or she saved per week. Next, these hours were multiplied by the standard values of dollars per hour ($75) and number of weeks per year (48). Then, all of the dollar benefits from the participants were tallied to produce the total of unqualified annualized benefits. Unqualified benefits are those benefits that have not been isolated as a result of the impact from the initiative. Annualized benefits must be qualified in order to be used in an ROI analysis.

QUALIFYING THE MONETARY BENEFITS

Qualifying monetary benefits is perhaps the most challenging aspect of bottom-line OD. The qualification process involves isolating the impact of the initiative on performance from all other potential influencing factors. Effectively isolating the effects of an initiative is determined by how the change plan is developed (Chapter 5), how pilots are conducted (Chapter 6), and how data are gathered and analyzed during deployment (Chapter 6). We are now at the point in the bottom-line OD process when all of these isolation considerations come together to produce credible, qualified monetary benefits.

In the case study example, one executive had produced $18,000 in (unqualified) benefits. End-user estimation was used as the only tool to isolate the impact of the initiative to produce these monetary benefits. Participants were asked to estimate the percentage of hours they saved per week that was directly a result of the initiative. Then each participant was asked to express, again on a percentage basis, his or her confidence in that estimate. The executive who produced $18,000 in benefits qualified these benefits as follows:

$$\$18,000 \times 50\% \text{ contribution} \times 80\% \text{ confidence} = \$7,200$$

Qualified benefits of $7,200 were added to the benefits total for the initiative.

Table 7.2 Summary of the Evaluation of a Sales Process Improvement Program for an Equipment Manufacturer

Background	Isolation Strategy	Monetary Conversion
Business goal: Increase contribution margins by 10% in two years	Established base period of one year for 600-B line sales before initiative launch.	The change in sales revenue from the base period to the post-initiative period for each salesperson was determined.
Initiative: Sales process improvement for a equipment manufacturer, including reengineering the sales process and conducting implementation workshops with sales people and managers	This base period was compared to a one-year post-initiative period that followed.	Sales revenue was discounted by a 17% margin rate.

Margin revenue changes were tallied for participants for both base and test periods. |
| *Evaluation objective:* Revenue margin increases in the 600-B line for initiative participants | Expert estimations were obtained from salespeople and sales managers. | Estimations of initiative impact made by salespeople and managers averaged to be 21%. |
| *Unit of Measure:* Output unit of "margins from 600-B line units sold" | Customers were interviewed to confirm the changes in behavior of the salespeople and the impact these changes had on their buying decisions. | Total change in revenue margin ($640,000) was multiplied by 21% to produce total benefits of $134,400. |

Evaluation in a Nutshell: Two Examples of Converting Benefits to Monetary Value

Evaluation activities of a strategic change initiative may span many months. These activities begin with the initial diagnosis and conclude well after initiative deployment. Now that the deployment team has disbanded, the donuts are stale, and the coffee is cold, it is the time to pull

Table 7.3 Summary of the Evaluation of a Quality Initiative for a Government Agency

Background	Isolation Strategy	Monetary Conversion
Organization goal: Move toward a service-oriented culture where employees go the extra mile to help customers	Track the trend-line of first-time call resolutions from the three months before the initiative to three months after the initiative.	Cost of quality is defined by the added transaction cost of every call multiple beyond the first call.
Initiative: Action learning workshops followed by manager reinforcement sessions		A standard monetary value is determined, on average, for a call that is not resolved the first time.
Evaluation objective: Achieve a 5% increase in first-time customer call resolution in six months	Managers conduct periodic audio monitoring of call center people to verify new culture behavior is evidenced.	Total call volume is tracked, resource availability is tracked, and first-time resolutions are tracked, as are multiple-call resolutions.
Unit of measure: Quality unit percent of customer calls resolved the first time		Trend-line analysis revealed a 4% increase in first-time resolutions, resulting in annual benefits of $780,000.

together all of the pieces of the evaluation puzzle. Table 7.2 summarizes the evaluation of a sales process improvement program for an equipment manufacturer. Table 7.3 does the same for a quality initiative of a governmental agency. These examples are intended to show what an integrated evaluation process looks like. The next two sections build on these examples to show how program costs are tabulated and the ROI calculated.

Coaching Return on Investment Study Cost Tabulation Worksheet

Instructions: Please use this worksheet to determine the total program costs for the coaching process. The purpose of this worksheet is to capture all of the costs associated with this project, including the time spent by the HR staff and the coaching clients. Many of the line items may not apply. If exact cost values for any particular line item are not known, please estimate on the high side of what you think was the true cost.

Diagnosis Costs
Salaries and benefits (everyone involved) _____
Meals, travel and associated expenses _____
Office supplies _____
Printing and reproduction _____
Electronic media _____
Outside services, consultants, vendors _____
Equipment expenses _____
General overhead allocations _____
Other miscellaneous expenses _____
   TOTAL _____ _____

Design and Development Costs
Salaries and benefits (everyone involved) _____
Meals, travel and associated expenses _____
Office supplies _____
Printing and reproduction _____
Electronic media _____
Outside services, consultants, vendors _____
Equipment expenses _____
General overhead allocations _____
Other miscellaneous expenses _____
   TOTAL _____ _____

Deployment Costs
Salaries and benefits (participants) _____
Salaries and benefits (facilitators) _____
Salaries and benefits (sponsors, governance) _____
Participant replacement costs _____
Other opportunity costs (e.g., lost sales, production, etc.) _____
Meals, travel and associated expenses _____
Office supplies _____
Printing and reproduction _____
Electronic media _____
Outside services, consultants, vendors _____
Equipment expenses _____
Facility costs (including company facilities) _____
General overhead allocations _____
Other miscellaneous expenses _____
   TOTAL _____ _____

Figure 7.1 Cost summary worksheet: Coaching ROI study.

Evaluation and Program Completion Costs
Salaries and benefits (everyone involved)   _____
Meals, travel and associated expenses   _____
Office supplies   _____
Printing and reproduction   _____
Electronic media   _____
Outside services, consultants, vendors   _____
Equipment expenses   _____
General overhead allocations   _____
Other miscellaneous expenses   _____
   TOTAL   _____   _____

TOTAL PROGRAM COSTS   _____

Figure 7.1 Continued

TABULATING THE COSTS OF THE INITIATIVE

Strategic change initiatives are complex and therefore require significant investment. This investment may take many forms: participants' time, opportunity costs, consulting fees, materials preparation, travel, and many other areas. Also, the total cost of the evaluation must be included in the analysis. This means that costs incurred beginning with the diagnosis and design of the initiative are included as well. It is clear that tabulating the total cost of an initiative is a gargantuan task. Many people must be solicited to contribute to the cost determination.

One approach that has been used successfully to gather initiative costs is to develop and distribute a cost survey. Figure 7.1 shows such a survey that was used to tabulate the costs of the coaching ROI case study presented in this book. In this case, the evaluator selected people from human resources and the coaching vendor to complete the cost tabulations. The evaluator verified the cost tabulations.

Amortization

One issue that often comes up with large strategic change initiatives is whether some costs should be spread out over a period greater than one year. Amortization is a commonly used tool to accomplish this task. Chapter 5 touched on this issue briefly. We will now look at this issue in more detail as it relates to tabulating costs. Accounting departments will have the guidelines for using amortization. The logic goes like this:

If say, a CD-ROM–based decision support tool for leaders will be used over a three-year period, then shouldn't only one year's worth of cost be factored in the cost tabulation? After all, we are looking only at the first year of benefits. The answer is: It depends. If doing so is within the accounting guidelines of the organization, then the answer is yes; however, all expected maintenance and upgrade costs must also be factored in. For software, this usually represents about 25% of the development cost per year.

Following this example for a CD-ROM that cost $100,000 to develop:

Without amortization   = $100,000
With (3-year) amortization = $100,000 + 25% (Year 2) + 25%
                             (Year 3) ÷ 3 Years = $50,000

In this case the cost was reduced (from $100,000 to $50,000), but some amortization schedules and accounting guidelines can be rather complicated, and there may be tax implications as well. Given this, it may just be best to include all of the cost as a first-year cost. This latter action, if taken, can be noted as an additional example of the conservative nature of the analysis.

Prorated vs. Direct Costs

Another issue that often arises is whether to prorate costs or to use direct costs. A prorated cost is one where the total cost of the initiative is divided by the number of participants. Then the cost for a given organization unit is determined by multiplying the number of participants in the organization unit by the prorated cost. Proration is appropriate when the initiative cost must be determined for a unit within the larger organization. The case study in Chapter 13 provides an example of using proration in determining the annual cost of a virtual, global community of practice dedicated to dealer service training:

- ☐ The total cost of the knowledge management capability was $.97 million.
- ☐ The total number of users of knowledge management was 15,000.
- ☐ The prorated cost per user of knowledge management was about $65.
- ☐ The number of practice members in the dealer community was 60.
- ☐ The prorated cost of the dealer community was $3900.

This is an appropriate use of proration because it would not be fair or accurate to match the monetary benefits of one community with the cost of the entire knowledge management capability.

Opportunity Costs

One decision that must be made is how to account for people's time while they were engaged in initiative activities. The most straightforward approach is to count the number of hours everyone spent on initiative activities, multiply this by the standard value for people's time, and voilá—you have captured this cost category. In some cases, especially with salespeople, the client or sponsor may call this approach into question. Salespeople, for example, are on commission, in some cases 100% commission. New salespeople are often working off a draw, which may vary from salesperson to salesperson. In any event, salespeople are compensated differently than other employees, so standard values will not work. A salesperson involved in an initiative is spending time in an activity that is not directly related to selling, and because of this it is likely that some sales will be lost. This is especially true with products with short sales cycles, such as automobiles. If the salesperson is not in the showroom when the prospective buyer walks in, then that sale will not happen, at least not for the missing salesperson.

Opportunity costs are calculated by first documenting the time that a person, we'll say a salesperson, spent in initiative activities. Then the average sales generated by that person for that given timeframe is determined. This monetary amount is discounted by the margin rate. This final amount is included with the program costs. When basing opportunity costs on lost sales, then the amount of time the person spent with the initiative is not counted. It is one or the other: lost sales or lost time, not both.

- ☐ Time that the salesperson spent in the initiative = 5 days
- ☐ Average sales generated in a five-day period = $35,000
- ☐ Margin rate (23%) discount = $8050

So $8050 of cost would be loaded into the cost tally. This is significantly greater than the $3000 that would be loaded if only the salesperson's time had been included ($75 per hour × 40 hours).

One last consideration here is that an argument can be made for many strategic initiative activities, that these activities are part of the salesperson's or sales manager's regular activities, and therefore calculating opportunity costs would not be appropriate. For example, an action learning session is a forum where salespeople develop their new marketing plans. Developing these plans is an integral part of their work and it should not matter where they do it—an action learning session or their offices. Therefore, because the salespeople would be doing this activity anyway, opportunity costs should not be taken. Some people might argue that *no* costs should be taken in this case. The point here is that some judgment and common sense are required. The evaluator and client or sponsor work together to make the right call.

CALCULATING THE RETURN ON INVESTMENT

Benefits have been determined, costs tabulated, and now it is time to calculate the return on investment. Actually, there are two commonly used (and sometimes confused) formulas: ROI and benefits/cost ratio (BCR).

Return on investment is calculated by:

$$((\text{Benefits} - \text{Costs}) \div \text{Costs}) \times 100$$

The benefits/cost ratio is determined by:

$$\text{Benefis} \div \text{Costs}$$

The primary difference is that ROI is based on *net* benefits, whereas the BCR is based on total benefits. Both calculations are useful in understanding the business value of a change initiative.

Let's turn to the two examples used earlier in this chapter to show how these calculations are made. The evaluation of the sales process improvement initiative for the equipment manufacturer produced total monetary benefits of $134,400. The total cost of the initiative was $120,000. The ROI and BCR were calculated as follows:

$$\text{ROI} = ((\$134,400 - \$120,000) \div \$120,000) \times 100 = 12\%$$

$$\text{BCR} = \$134,400 \div \$120,000 = 1.1:1$$

Are the ROI of 12% and BCR of 1.1:1 good or bad? How do we interpret these numbers? In this case, the expectation of the business unit leader was that revenue margins would increase by 10% in two years. Let's keep in mind that the study only looked at benefits for the first year, not the second year. So in this sense the evaluation is not yet complete, at least in the mind of the business leader, because it would be important to look at second-year benefits. Also, the emphasis is on sales margin increase and not so much on how this increase was produced. The BCR says that for every dollar invested in the change initiative, $1.10 will be returned. Basically, the initiative pays for itself. Sales margins did increase by 7% in the first year, so the business leader is pleased that the organization is well on its way toward achieving its business goal. Having the initiative cover its own costs is just icing on the cake. Let's turn to the second example, the evaluation of a quality initiative for a government agency. Here, the benefits were $780,000 and program costs were $260,000. The ROI and BCR calculations were as follows:

$$ROI = ((\$780,000 - \$260,000) \div \$260,000) \times 100 = 200\%$$

$$BCR = \$780,000 \div \$260,000 = 3:1$$

At first blush this looks like a successful initiative. This initiative produced $3 for every dollar invested and a 200% ROI. It is hard to argue with this kind of ROI; however, let us put this ROI in the context of the organization goal. This goal was to "move toward a service-oriented culture where employees go the extra mile to help customers." This culture change was measured in part by first-time call resolutions. The 4% gain in first-time call resolutions fell short of the 5% objective. The $780,000 in benefits, while impressive, is a means to an end, not the end itself. Culture change is what is needed, and so far the initiative appeared to fall short of this goal.

What can be done at this point? It is clear from the analysis that there is real money in reducing the number of customer transactions. Increasing first-time call resolutions does reduce the total number of transactions. The initiative therefore has produced monetary benefits that open additional investment options. The action learning workshops can be expanded or manager reinforcement sessions enhanced. It is also possible that the initiative has delivered about as much as it can deliver to effect culture change. Another avenue for investment may be to conduct another, more focused diagnosis on ferreting out root cause issues. For example, the secondary diagnosis may reveal that the sheer amount of information required by each call center representative to resolve a wide range of issues on the first call is too great and too hard to remember. Then the answer may be to reengineer the work process. A skill-based routing process, for example, may have to be implemented whereby representatives specialize in certain areas of expertise and customers navigate a series of menus to access the right expertise.

The point to be made here is that the ROI calculation is not the end of the exploration process; rather, it is the beginning. Clients, initiative sponsors, governance groups, and many others must be engaged in exploring the information, gaining critical knowledge about the initiative and the implications for the organization, and applying their new-found wisdom to achieving even greater organization success. The change practitioner and the evaluation specialist are responsible for leading everyone through this journey.

How to Build Credibility for an ROI Analysis

The ROI analysis, no matter how well conceived and executed, will have little impact if it is perceived to lack credibility. Credibility is a judgment, and judgments are based on perceptions. It is critical, therefore, for change practitioners and evaluators to appropriately manage these perceptions. This is especially true in organizations that have not had much experience with evaluating ROI of strategic change initiatives. Figure 7.2 illustrates seven practical steps that can be taken to build credibility of the ROI analysis.

1. *Continue to emphasize the link of the evaluation to the top business goal.* Memories fade and organizational myopia sets in. The good work done during the initial stages of the initiative to develop evaluation objectives with a clear line of sight to the top goals of the organization will pay big dividends toward the end of the initiative. The performance of the evaluation objectives has a direct impact on the organization achieving its goals. Frame the results in this context. Remind business leaders about how the initiative will impact the business. Ensure that business leaders grasp the implications of the initiative and how it will be evaluated for the business. Evaluation results gain credibility as these results affect decisions regarding achieving top organization goals.

2. *Early in the initiative, identify and work closely with the key financial person.* Virtually every leader and leadership team has at least one (and often just one) financial person who can be relied on to review and produce reliable and accurate numbers. Find out who this person is and buy him or her lunch periodically. Review all

Figure 7.2 Building credibility for an ROI analysis.

of the evaluation plans, steps, calculations, and draft reports with this person. If he or she supports the evaluation, then the evaluation will gain a tremendous amount of credibility.

3. *Be conservative at each step, and note these conservative steps.* Evaluating strategic change is a conservative process: Only annualized and qualified benefits are used and compared with fully loaded costs. Evaluation decisions always take the most conservative path. It is important not only to make these decisions, but also to highlight that these conservative decisions have been made. People reading the evaluation report will see at each step how the most conservative approach was taken, and the report will gain credibility with each step. When business leaders begin complaining that the approach is too conservative and the resulting ROIs are too low, you know you have hit the mark.

4. *Utilize the most reputable sources in the analysis.* Data are only as credible as the source from which they are drawn. Credible sources (generally) produce credible data. The opposite is also true. Sources not perceived by others to be credible will not produce data that are perceived to be credible. Share your sources

during the evaluation process with the client or initiative sponsor. He or she will say if additional sources are required and where credible data may be located. This issue is most pronounced when dealing with estimates. Only people perceived as credible can make credible estimates. Use third-party sources to verify estimates whenever possible.

5. *Use multiple measures when isolating the effects of the initiative.* Often, the credibility of the entire evaluation boils down to people's acceptance of how the effects of the initiative were isolated. It is essential to use as many methods as possible to isolate the effects from other potential influences on the results. Credibility grows with the results of each isolation method. Pre-/post-initiative studies, the use of comparison groups, and having a rich diversity of estimations are all factors in building credibility.

6. *Circulate a discussion draft of the ROI report before issuing the final report.* Every ROI report will have judgments, estimations, assumptions, and other gray areas that people may react to. It is important to allow these people to voice their concerns in a way that does not impinge on the credibility of the report. Issuing a discussion draft of the report to all constituents for review is an effective way of gaining their input. This approach will not only limit the potential loss of credibility, but it will actually increase the credibility of the final report. People will tend to buy in to a report to which they have contributed. Incorporating their edits and ideas will strengthen the report and greatly increase its credibility. Be sure to clearly identify the document as a discussion draft (or equivalent language) and specifically ask for input and ideas.

7. *Ensure the perceived independence of the evaluator.* An evaluator who is perceived, rightly or wrongly, to have a stake in the outcome of the evaluation will not be viewed as credible. Consequently, the credibility of the ROI report will suffer. Utilizing an external evaluator is the clearest choice to ensure the independence of the evaluator, but it is also an expensive choice. Consideration can be given to utilizing someone from quality assurance or a Six Sigma team to conduct the evaluation. The finance function is another source. This person would be independent of the organizational group that is responsible for the initiative. Another

possibility is to create a small evaluation team of, say, three people each drawn from human resources, finance, and quality assurance. The team would then sign off on all evaluation decisions. Most organization leaders would view this approach as credible. The simplest approach may be just to ask the client or sponsor who the most credible evaluator would be and to go with his or her recommendation.

LEVERAGING STRATEGIC INSIGHTS

Not effectively communicating and leveraging the evaluation of a successful initiative is like snatching defeat from the jaws of victory. Yet, so often people do not adequately communicate the results of the evaluation to the organization. Evaluations create knowledge. Evaluations of strategic change initiatives create strategic knowledge. This knowledge can be leveraged to enhance the competitive advantage of the organization and improve its chances of success in achieving strategic goals. There are several ways to leverage knowledge in the organization.

Develop Key Strategic Messages Based on the ROI Results

Strategic change initiatives are high-visibility efforts, and communicating the results also must have equally high visibility. People, and perhaps especially Americans, respond to soundbite-sized messages. These are short, punchy, meaningful messages that can be swallowed and digested easily. Different audiences require, or can at least absorb, different messages. Key messages for the senior leadership group may be different from messages issued for general consumption. It is important, therefore, to target messages to specific audiences.

Returning to the case study involving the government agency, a key message for the leadership team may have been "we have not yet hit the bedrock of culture change." This message would open dialogue and direct the leadership team to explore other potential initiatives to achieve the organization goal of culture change. At least this message might open the door for further inquiry and diagnosis into root cause issues. This particular message, however, might be discouraging to customer call center people who are feeling good about the progress they have made. A message more like "we're making change happen!" would recognize the progress that is being made and yet imply that more work and change are needed. Most organizations have communications professionals who can help develop and refine these messages for specific audiences.

Make Available a Common Set of Communication Materials

Consistency is the key when communicating messages. People who hear different messages or who detect inconsistencies in the messages they hear will quickly become confused. Strategic communication is not a jazz ensemble; it is a carefully orchestrated symphony, although a symphony with ample audience participation (e.g., two-way communications). A common set of communication materials can be developed along the lines of the key messages. These materials are made available to every appropriate person who needs them. These materials include slide presentations, a list of frequently asked questions with answers, and talking points for leaders and managers to discuss the results of the initiative.

Another effective tool is to create a set of representative stories illustrating behavior and culture change that came about as a result of the initiative. Stories are powerful, partly because people can easily relate to the experiences of others and the emotional context of the story. For example, in the case of the government agency, a story could be written about someone who went above and beyond the call of duty to quickly resolve an urgent customer issue. This story would serve as a role model for others about what behaving in the new culture is all about in terms that they can easily relate to.

Open Two-Way Communications

Earlier, strategic communication was likened to a symphony orchestra, although one with audience participation. The audience participation in this case is created with two-way communications. Town hall meetings can be led by organization leaders who will share information and engage a variety of people in dialogue and answer questions. If technology is available, these town hall meetings can go online with Web-based interactive sessions. A community of practice or chat room can be established in the knowledge management system to foster give-and-take communications. If this technology is not available, telephone conference calls can be conducted.

Strategic change requires the energy and engagement of everyone in the organization. These communication activities are intended to focus people's energy and engage them on what is most strategically critical for the organization. Utilizing these activities to reward and recognize achievement will go a long way toward keeping people energized.

Open the Dialogue to Those Outside the Organization

Strategic change is all-inclusive. Creating a "big tent" for those outside the organization to become engaged in the change effort can be a powerful way to put more wind in the sails of change. Customers, suppliers, contractors, and other business partners can be included in the communication activities. Key messages can be developed for them that convey the essence of the new role they need to play in achieving mutual success. The value chain is strengthened as each link is reinforced with strategic communication activities.

SECTION TWO

Special Issues

This section deals with three important issues for strategic change valuation. The first issue is how to forecast ROI. Forecasting ROI is touched on in several parts in this book, and its importance as an evaluation tool warrants its own chapter. Forecasting ROI is gaining increased favor with change practitioners and business leaders are coming to expect this information in order to make decisions about proceeding with change initiatives. Change initiatives are being evaluated as a potential investment like any other business investment. The playing field is being leveled, and this chapter shows how to play the ROI game.

The second issue is how best to use surveys to collect ROI data. Virtually every ROI evaluation will employ some type of survey. Surveys allow a great deal of data to be collected in a timely and efficient way. This chapter deals with how to best use surveys to collect data about initiative benefits and, in particular, how to use surveys to isolate the effects of the initiative.

The third topic deals with ROI "on the fly," or how to conduct a post-initiative evaluation after pretty much ignoring evaluation throughout the entire implementation of the initiative. Post-initiative evaluations are often, and hastily, initiated when the CEO asks the change practitioner what value a recently completed initiative contributed to the business. This chapter provides a practical and straightforward approach to answer the CEO's question.

CHAPTER 8

Forecasting ROI

BUSINESS CONTEXT OF FORECASTING ROI FOR STRATEGIC CHANGE

In the business world, ROI calculations are mostly forecasts. Business leaders are constantly faced with making decisions about whether to invest in business improvement initiatives. They rely upon the forecast of the return they are likely to receive on the proposed investment. ROI is a decision-making tool. Business leaders must make choices. With a limited amount of investment capital, which investment will have the biggest bang for the buck? Into this mix of business initiatives comes proposals for strategic change initiatives. Forecasting ROI for strategic change initiatives levels the playing field. Investment decisions about strategic change initiatives may now be made in the same way that decisions about other business initiatives are settled.

Forecasting the ROI of strategic change typically encounters one major drawback: Business leaders have so little experience with determining the ROI of strategic change initiatives that they have a built-in skepticism about the potential returns. Nonetheless, properly done, forecasting the ROI of strategic change initiatives has many advantages:

☐ Decisions to invest in strategic change initiatives are based on expected business impact and not on fluffy notions of intangible value.

☐ Clear expectations of value can be set with the senior business leaders, and these expectations are a two-way street. Leaders will need to own up to their accountabilities to make the change successful. Achieving the ROI is largely placed in their hands.

☐ Everyone knows what the prize is. The financial ROI will literally be banked on. Cash flow projections, enhanced revenue streams, and fixed cost reductions will be expected to materialize based on the ROI forecast of the strategic change initiative.

By leveling the playing field, the onus is placed on the change practitioners to deliver tangible business value. Change practitioners and business leaders strengthen their partnership in making significant improvements to the business. ROI raises the ante and opens up new opportunities for partnership between change practitioners and business leaders. All eyes are on the change practitioner to set the ROI agenda. Now the change practitioners need to step up and make the big play.

Bottom-line OD takes the forecasting process one step further. Forecasting ROI for strategic change initiatives is not only a powerful tool for understanding the potential value of strategic initiatives, but it also becomes a tool for increasing the value of these initiatives. Forecasting is certainly a predictive tool to make decisions about how best to invest in strategic change initiatives, but the forecasting process introduces a level of discipline and business focus that leads to increasing the value of the strategic initiative. In contrast to how forecasting is used in other business decisions, bottom-line OD gut-checks the assumptions and, when the initiative has been deployed, determines the actual ROI. Let's face it, in these challenging business times, the more limited the availability of resources, money, and people, the more important it is to forecast potential value.

The beauty of forecasting ROI for strategic change is how readily ROI assumptions can be translated into expectations for business leaders to support the strategic change initiative. One assumption for gaining an ROI from a strategic change initiative is the level of participation of people in the initiative. The more the merrier. As each participant contributes his or her share of the monetary benefits, increasing the number of participants increases the benefits. Likewise, as more participants apply the lessons of strategic change to their work, the greater the monetary impact on the business. This dynamic duo—participation and application—represents the fundamental assumptions of the ROI forecast and the primary expectations of business leaders to deliver the goods. If, for example, our ROI is relying upon 80% of the people in the target population to participate in the initiative, then participation rates of less than 80% will reduce the ROI. If the ROI depends upon

60% of people applying the major tenants of the initiative to their work, then anything less than 60% reduces the ROI. All business leaders are responsible to satisfy these assumptions and meet these expectations to achieve the prize.

We will see, later in this chapter, how the ROI equation is amended to account for rates of participation and application. Tracking both of these rates during deployment enables leaders and change practitioners to conduct "what-if" scenarios to better understand—and better manage —the ROI of the change initiative.

REQUIREMENTS FOR FORECASTING

Forecasting cannot be attempted unless the following conditions are met: linkage, value, cost, and isolation.

1. ***Linkage.*** *There must be explicit linkage from the business goal to the strategic change objectives.* Forecasting ROI of an initiative implies that the initiative, if deployed successfully, will create tangible monetary value for the business. Credibility for the ROI forecast, then, depends on the credibility of the link from the initiative to the business. The link from the initiative to the business goal must be made explicit. This is nothing more than just good consulting practice.

2. ***Value.*** *The consultant and client must be able to make some assumptions about the value to be gained from the initiative.* The ROI forecast requires that the value be expressed in monetary terms. Given that the change has not happened, the monetary value must be estimated. The foundation of every estimate consists of assumptions. Assumptions underlying the strategic change initiatives address issues of how well leaders sustain their commitment to the initiative and how well people apply their new knowledge and behavior to their work. These assumptions are translated into expectations to deliver value to the business.

3. ***Cost.*** *There must be an understanding of the level of investments required to design and deploy the initiative.* Forecasting the ROI requires estimating the denominator (cost) of the ROI equation as well as the benefits. Estimating cost is usually more easily done than estimating the benefits, partly because more is known about the cost of the initiative. Decisions are made early in the design phase of the initiative that bear on deployment strategy, the

Table 8.1 Forecasting ROI During Phase 1 (Diagnosis) and Phase 3 (Development)

Phase	Business Question	Data Sources	Pluses and Minuses
1	Should we invest in the change initiative?	Archival data, similar initiatives recently completed, business performance data, cost estimates	+ Minimum investment at this point − Estimates on value and cost based mostly on assumptions
3	How best can we deploy the change initiative?	Data sources above, plus: accurate cost data, pilot data showing application and preliminary results	+ Decisions are made about deploying the initiative to maximize ROI − Substantial investment already made

population of participants, the use of vendors, timing, and other resource issues that have a bearing on investments. The investments can be fairly accurately estimated, with some assumptions, and tabulated to produce the total cost of the initiative.

4. *Isolation. There must be an agreed upon benchmark or process to isolate the potential impact of the initiative on performance.* Forecasts operate under the same rules for isolation as post-initiative ROI calculations (see Chapter 5). Forecasts require the potential monetary benefits to be directly attributable to the change initiative and isolated from other potential influencing factors. The need to isolate benefits is the same, whether it is done in a forecast or at the end of the initiative. One advantage of forecasting ROI is that the change practitioner and the client agree up front about the appropriate strategy to isolate the effects of the initiative. Therefore, as the initiative progresses there are no further questions or significant challenges about the appropriateness of the isolation process. Isolation is a big hurdle, and the sooner that it can be overcome the better.

TIMING OF ROI FORECASTS

The timing of the ROI forecast depends on the business question that the client and change practitioner would like to have answered (Table 8.1). There are two main questions that business leaders have on their minds. The first question deals with whether the initiative should be invested in at all. This question generally arises during Phase 1, the diagnostics phase. Occasionally, this question will pop up after the initiative has been deployed. All available data are assembled in the business case (Chapter 3) that lays out the arguments for moving forward. The ROI forecast is one data point that can strengthen the case for investing in the initiative. Recommendations are made. Business leaders decide on making the investment. If they decide that a change initiative is not going to deliver sufficient value to the organization, then it is good to know this now before further investments are made in designing and developing the initiative.

The second question that business leaders may ask is: Should the initiative be deployed? They have made the investment in designing and developing the initiative, and faced with imminent deployment, they may get cold feet. Canceling an initiative at this point would be a costly decision. After all, they have made a substantial investment to get to this point. Often, the question revolves around how best to deploy, not whether to deploy. An ROI forecast done during Phase 3 (Development) is best based on pilot data. The pilot provides real-world data about how the initiative fared in the organization. Although the number of participants in a pilot is low, these participants are fairly representative of the greater population. As such, pilot data carry a lot of weight with business leaders. These data support decisions facing business leaders about how to deploy the initiative more effectively. For example, the pilot may offer ideas about how to lower the costs of deployment or suggest the most effective sequence of business units for deploying the initiative.

Forecasting ROI follows the same five-step process, regardless of when it is done during the course of the initiative. How the steps are completed and the quality of the data differ for these two approaches. In general, the later in the change process the forecast is done, the better the data on which to base the forecast. Better data produce a better and more accurate forecast. Of course, the earlier the forecast is done, the greater its utility as a tool for making investment decisions. As the initiative rolls along, investments are made and cannot be recovered. ROI forecasting can really be done at any time. For example, sometimes the ROI is forecast during deployment as a tool to better shepherd the benefits to the bottom line. This chapter focuses on the two most prevalent junctures to forecast ROI.

This five-step process to forecast ROI includes the following:

1. Estimate benefits
2. Estimate investments

3. Determine ranges for participation and application
4. Forecast the ROI
5. Make recommendations

ROI forecasting for both Phase 1 and Phase 3 is explained according to this five-step process. Then a case study is presented that explores in detail how to forecast ROI.

PHASE 1 FORECAST: SHOULD WE INVEST IN THE CHANGE INITIATIVE?

The sooner that business leaders can make a decision about investing in an initiative, the better. The cost meter is running as soon as resources are committed to diagnosing organization issues, and these costs can mount quickly. If the initiative is ultimately not going to be pursued, then pulling the plug as soon as possible will limit the cost sunk into the initiative. It comes down to whether the total monetary benefit looks large enough to warrant the investment. The ROI forecast is conducted during proposal development after the results of the diagnosis are known. The forecast is featured in the business case, although the data supporting the forecast may be skimpy. Other than the use of archival data, there is often very little to go on other than conjecture and estimations. For this reason, the credibility of the ROI forecast for people and change initiatives can be called into question. Sometimes a range of ROI can be drawn based on best-case and worst-case scenarios. This approach will often appease the credibility critics.

The Five-Step Forecasting Process Conducted during Phase 1

The five steps to conduct a Phase 1 ROI forecast are accomplished as follows:

1. *Estimate Benefits.* Archival data are reviewed to estimate a range of potential benefits. Archival data includes information about the impact of similar initiatives to produce tangible value and tracking business performance data. External benchmarks drawn from published studies may also be used to estimate benefits. External consultants often have experience implementing similar strategic change projects for other clients, and these data can be used to estimate value. Ballpark estimates are the norm. Previous experience or recently completed initiatives within the organization or

with similar organizations can be drawn on to estimate a range of benefits. Assumptions underlying the estimates are noted.

2. *Estimate cost.* The total expected cost of the initiative is estimated. This cost includes all of the cost elements described in Chapter 7. Assumptions are noted.

3. *Determine ranges for participation and application.* The change practitioner, sponsor, and business leaders will agree on acceptable ranges for rates of participation and application. While 100% participation of people in the change initiative would be ideal, it is rarely achieved in reality. People in the target population may go on vacation, be out on sick leave, or may opt out of the initiative at the last moment. In the worst case, business leaders may cite challenging business conditions as a pretext to withdraw a significant portion of their organizations from participating in the initiative. Generally, 80% to 95% are realistic participation rates.

   People rarely utilize all of the new knowledge and behaviors that they gain from a strategic change initiative, at least not right away. Most organizations that have put into place accountability mechanisms for ensuring people apply what they have learned realize application rates in the range of 50% to 70%. In part, this relates to how "application" is operationally defined. The question that often comes up is: "Does application mean the percent of *people* who have applied the material, or the percent of *material* applied by each person?" The answer is both. For example, at Braxton Industries, they defined application as the "percent of leaders who successfully used the five-step coaching process within six weeks of workshop completion." This definition embraces people (percent of leaders), content (five-step coaching process), and timing (within six weeks). All three of these elements must be included in any operational definition of application.

4. *Forecast ROI.* A range of potential ROIs is calculated based on the range of benefits estimated earlier. The assumptions made about participation, application, and other areas play a major role in the forecasting process. The ROI forecast can change dramatically as decisions made by the client and governance team affect these assumptions. It is important, in these cases, to factor these changes into the ROI equation and restate the forecast. In this way, the forecasting process shows the financial implications of these decisions. These what-if scenarios can be helpful in max-

imizing the use of resources for the initiative and making the best decisions for the business. The ROI equation is amended to factor in rates for participation and application:

$$ROI\ (F) = ((BENEFITS - COST) \div COST) \times 100 \\ \times PARTICIPATION \times APPLICATION$$

5. *Make recommendations.* The main recommendation at this point is whether to proceed with the initiative. The approval to proceed can be conditional. That is, approval may be given to proceed through the design phase and then, at that point, to reevaluate the status of the initiative.

PHASE 3 FORECAST: SHOULD WE PROCEED WITH FULL DEPLOYMENT?

At this point, the initiative has been designed and developed. This means that there is much better information about the expected benefits and the investments required to deploy the initiative. Given the strategic nature of the initiative, one or more pilots will most likely be conducted. If pilots are to be conducted, then this opens some possibilities for collecting additional data for the forecast. The key data here are application (level 3) data. Pilot application data point to how people have utilized what they learned to create results for the business. Participants in the strategic change pilots can estimate, on a percentage basis, how much their effectiveness will likely be improved. Areas of business improvement can be identified and estimates used to show the expected financial value of deploying the initiative.

The five-step process described earlier is again employed to conduct an ROI forecast during Phase 3. Incorporating pilot data into the forecast increases the accuracy and credibility of the ROI calculations. More accurate cost data are available as well. The Phase 3 forecast will be illustrated with a case study.

CASE STUDY: FORECASTING ROI AT BRAXTON INDUSTRIES

The leaders at Braxton Industries were committed to improving performance management. Given the size and scope of the investment, they wanted a forecast of the potential ROI. Table 8.2 summarizes the approach to forecasting the ROI. It was decided to conduct the forecast based on the results of the pilot. This kind of initiative had never been attempted at this company before, so there was little previous data or

Table 8.2 Forecasting ROI at Braxton Industries

Evaluation Objectives	Data Collection During Pilot	Isolating Effects	Forecasting Benefits
Increased achievement of sales goals attributable to performance management (PM)	Reaction and learning comprehension data collected via in-session questionnaire to each participant. Application data collected via e-mail survey administered 4–6 weeks after pilot. Conduct selected third-party follow-up.	End-user estimation of: 1. How PM was applied 2. Impact on sales goal(s) 3. Determine any increased revenue 4. Convert to monetary value 5. Estimate contribution of PM to produce benefits 6. Express confidence in estimate (error factor)	1. Tally monetary benefits of all participants. 2. Project range of benefits for entire population. 3. State assumptions for range of projection. 4. Determine total program cost for companywide deployment. 5. Forecast ROIs. 6. Capture intangible benefits. 7. Make recommendations for PM deployment.

experiences on which to rely. The pilot data would yield enough reliable information that would support the ROI forecast.

Estimate Benefits

Data collected during the pilot included the participants' reaction to the new performance management process and how well they learned the new process and new behavior. A survey of participants was conducted immediately after the pilot. This survey enabled participants to isolate the effects of the initiative. Participants were asked how much more effective they would be in managing their salespeople as a result of applying the new performance management process. An assumption was made that more effectively managing salespeople will increase the ability of the salespeople to sell more equipment. How much more effective? Participants made the estimation as follows:

☐ Participants (24) in the pilots estimated that they would be 35% more effective in managing the performance of their salespeople. They were 80% confident in this estimation. Therefore, participants estimated that they would be 28% more effective after the error factor is considered (35% × 80%).

☐ Participants estimated that their improved performance would increase the performance of their salespeople (85) by 42%. They were 70% confident in this estimate to produce an estimate of improved salesperson performance of 29% (42% × 70%).

☐ How much of this improved performance would translate to increased sales? Participants estimated that improved performance would increased sales by 40%.

☐ The total sales of the participants' sales force of the preceding year were $146 million.

☐ The margins on these sales were (on average) 17%.

☐ The total revenue margin for the sales force was $25 million ($146 M × 17%).

Pulling together all of these pieces will produce the expected monetary benefits attributed to the performance management initiative. The formula is as follows:

Revenue Margins
    × increased manager's effectiveness (includes isolation and error)
    × increased performance of salespeople (includes isolation and error)
    × increased sales resulting from improved performance
    = expected monetary benefits

Applying this formula to the data runs as follows:

$$\$25 \text{ million} \times 28\% \times 29\% \times 40\% = \$812,000$$

This means that the initiative is expected to produce monetary benefits of $812,000.

Estimate Cost

The total program cost of the initiative was expected to be $600,000. This cost figure included all costs incurred to date (e.g., diagnosis, design, development), as well as all costs expected from the deployment, evaluation, and communication activities of the initiative.

Determine Participation and Application Rates

The initiative sponsor and the Vice President of Sales estimated (and committed to) participation rates in the range of 70% to 95% and achieving application rates of 60% to 80%.

Underlying these assumptions about rates is the continued support and commitment of the Vice President of Sales and other leaders to improve performance management. For example, the Vice President of Sales must ensure that all Sales managers actively participate in the initiative and that they apply their new skills and knowledge to achieve the upper range of the ROI forecast.

Forecast the ROI

Given this investment level, the range of ROIs was forecasted as follows:

$$((\$812{,}000 - \$600{,}000) \div \$600{,}000) \times 100 \times 95\% \times 80\% = 27\%$$

$$((\$812{,}000 - \$600{,}000) \div \$600{,}000) \times 100 \times 95\% \times 60\% = 20\%$$

$$((\$812{,}000 \quad \$600{,}000) \div \$600{,}000) \times 100 \times 70\% \times 80\% = 20\%$$

$$((\$812{,}000 - \$600{,}000) \div \$600{,}000) \times 100 \times 70\% \times 60\% = 15\%$$

Many intangible benefits were also noted during the collection of pilot data. These included increased customer satisfaction, improved morale of salespeople, and stronger teamwork.

Make Recommendations

The ROI forecast generated a great deal of interest and discussion. The message to the business leadership was clear: the ball is in your court. In other words, achieving the higher end of the range of benefits depends on their sustained commitment to the initiative. Specific recommendations included:

- ☐ Leadership must sustain this commitment to the initiative through-out deployment to ensure high manager participation rates.

- ☐ Leaders must also regularly follow up with managers to ensure that they are applying new skills and knowlege from the initiative to the work environment.

- ☐ Leaders should, to accomplish the first two recommendations, personally participate in the initiative and be seen as active, visible sponsors of the change effort.

- ☐ Initiative managers must aggressively look at expenditures and manage the investment level of the initiative.

These recommendations are largely based on the assumptions that were made to achieve monetary benefits. These recommendations become in effect the *de facto* expectations for the role that leaders must play. For example, a leader whose business unit is falling behind in participation rates during the deployment phase is, according to the ROI forecast, jeopardizing the prize. Lower participation rates will point to the lower end of the range of benefits described in the ROI forecast. The implication here is not very subtle. Leaders who waver in their support of the initiative reduce the business benefits. Leadership behavior will determine whether the initiative generates a return, breaks even, or is a drain on cash flow.

The ROI forecast also highlights another important aspect of ROI: cost. If the cost of the initiative seems too high for the expected benefits, the initiative managers can look for ways to save money. Deployment represents fertile ground for saving money. In this case study example, deployment featured a series of face-to-face workshops. This approach drove up costs. The question is: Are there other less costly ways of accomplishing the same implementation objective? Could the e-learning, for example, be utilized instead of face-to-face workshops? Lowering cost during deployment will yield higher ROIs given the same level of benefits.

What Happens if the ROI Forecast Is Negative?

Well, for starters, this can be a very good thing. Most business leaders would rather have their bad news come in a forecast rather than the reality of their business results. In fact, this is largely the problem that most business leaders face today: They do not find out how an initiative benefited (or did not benefit) the business until well after the initiative has been deployed. Knowing that a change initiative will likely not produce the expected financial return requires actions that will benefit the business and ultimately produce more business leaders who are satisfied that the change initiative met their expectations. These actions include the following:

1. *Stopping the initiative and redirecting resources.* Business leaders may decide to cut their losses. Those who were working on the initiative would be redeployed to other work or other initiatives. This is not a total loss—really far from it. The leaders have learned a great deal about the organization, its people, and work processes, and also have learned what works or what doesn't work in the organization. The possibility remains open that, when business conditions change, the initiative can be resurrected.

2. *Rescoping the initiative to increase the ROI.* The forecast can open people's eyes to making significant improvements in the initiative. These improvements can increase the ROI. In the case of Braxton Industries, finding an effective alternative to the face-to-face workshops represented an opportunity to reduce the costs of the initiative. Improvements can be made to increase the benefits. For example, the applied coaching and feedback portion of the change initiative can be expanded to increase managerial effectiveness to a level higher than 42%. Increased effectiveness of managers will lead to increased benefits for the business.

3. *Proceeding with the initiative with a clearer understanding of the benefits.* The ROI forecast is a great learning tool. Forecasting requires people to examine, and even to challenge, the assumptions they are making about the initiative. Leaders have a clearer idea about their role in supporting the initiative. Change practitioners have gained a much deeper understanding about how the initiative will deliver bottom-line business results.

BENEFITS OF THE ROI FORECAST

The ROI forecast is a powerful tool to not only understand how much monetary value a change initiative will deliver, but also to increase this value. Benefits of forecasting ROI include:

- ☐ *Improved decision making about whether to invest in an initiative.* The ROI forecast is a proven decision-making tool. Business leaders appreciate having forecast information on which to base investment decisions. Forecasting produces higher-quality data, which leads to higher-quality decision making. Making a decision on a change initiative based in part on ROI data enables leaders to measure all initiatives—business improvement and strategic change initiatives—with a common yardstick. Understanding the expected monetary business results provides a good footing for setting priorities.

- ☐ *Increased leadership commitment to deploy the initiative.* Forecast data are based on assumptions. Best-case and worst-case scenarios illustrate how these assumptions are likely to play out during initiative deployment. Leaders now have additional insight and some levers to pull so that the best-case scenario can be realized. Their commitment to the initiative increases as they take actions to increase the value of the initiative.

- ☐ *Clearer expectations for people's role in strategic change.* Forecasting helps people understand how their role in the initiative leads to creating bottom-line value for the organization. People also improve their understanding of other people's role in the initiative. People can set much clearer expectations for one another that are rooted in delivering value. Expectations are not only clearer, but they are also higher than if forecasting was not done. Every player on the team knows what he or she must do to score and win the game.

- ☐ *Improved management of cost and benefit factors.* ROI forecasts make predictions about how much investment an initiative will require to produce certain monetary benefits. If people don't like the answer, they have two major options to change the ROI calculation: (1) lower the expected cost of the initiative, which will increase the ROI; or (2) increase the expected benefits, resulting in a higher ROI. Both of these courses of action improve the ability of the initiative to deliver value to the business. By taking these courses of action, leaders and change practitioners improve their management of the initiative.

Tricks of the Trade: Using Surveys to Collect ROI Data

The change population is large; the change practitioners are few. The need for data is great. What do we do? The answer to this question is invariably to conduct survey research. Surveys have proven to be an effective and relatively quick way to gain insights about a wide range of organizational issues. The ROI issue is no different. Strategic change practitioners must understand how to best use survey research to gather reliable ROI data. Developing effective questionnaires and surveys, providing insightful analysis of the data, and ferreting out the most salient and meaningful conclusions from the data are essential skills for every change practitioner.

A lot has been learned about how to use surveys to gather ROI data, and there are special challenges. This chapter shares pragmatic experiences that address the most critical ROI issues. Readers will gain increased competence in utilizing research methodology for ROI analysis and confidence in discussing ROI data with clients. The questions that this chapter will address are:

- [ ] Why is survey research essential for ROI analysis?
- [ ] What are the limitations of survey research for ROI analysis?
- [ ] What is the fastest, easiest way to use surveys to isolate the effects of the initiative?
- [ ] How can response rates be increased?
- [ ] What are the essential elements of ROI questionnaire construction?

Why Is Survey Research Essential for ROI Analysis?

Surveys have three main advantages for collecting ROI data: speed, efficiency, and consistency. Surveys can be used to collect large amounts of data in a relatively short period. With the advent of the Internet, surveys may be administered electronically around the world. Software is available that allows surveys to be posted on Internet sites, then respondents access the site and complete the survey online, and the software automatically tabulates and analyzes the data according to the instructions given by the researcher. Data consistency is assured because all respondents are asked the same questions. Surveys can be constructed in a few hours, meaning that a great deal of data is produced with a minimum of effort by the researcher.

Practically all estimation data are gathered with surveys. Estimations gain credibility as more people provide data. Estimations of the effect of a change initiative on a business indicator will have more credibility if the estimation is based on the input of 40 managers vs. 4 managers. Surveys enable the researcher to gather the data from 40 managers quickly and consistently. Evaluating people's initial reaction to the change (level 1), how well they have learned the requirements for change (level 2), how well they are applying what they have learned (level 3), and how their new actions affect the business (level 4) can all be determined with surveys. Determining the ROI (level 5) is on much stronger footing with survey data.

What Are the Limitations of Survey Research for ROI Analysis?

ROI analysis imposes some limitations on the use of surveys. First, respondents likely have little knowledge about how to isolate the effects of their experiences, convert these experiences to monetary benefits, and perform other ROI procedures. This means that the survey questions (or items) will have to be detailed and offer a step-by-step approach for respondents. The challenge is to provide these steps in a way that is not too onerous, time consuming, or confusing to respondents. If so, respondents will just quit responding and move on to something else. Completing a survey is usually done privately, so there is little opportunity to ask questions along the way.

The nature of ROI questions can be perceived as challenging in and of themselves. Producing monetary benefits implies personal value to the organization, especially at higher levels in an organization. What executive wants to complete a questionnaire in which it is clear that he or she produced no monetary value as the result of the change initiative? Also, executives play "show me yours and I'll show you mine" games to see who provided the most monetary value to the business. Data integrity can be an issue here as well. Respondents who perceive a vested interest in showing monetary results may be tempted to puff up their contributions.

A more general concern is survey fatigue. Surveys are so frequently administered in organizations that employees are reluctant, and in some cases even resentful, about taking additional surveys. People's time is at a premium, and they view the time they take with the survey as time that is taken away from other responsibilities. Surveys that are perceived as taking too long to complete will be less likely to be completed and returned to the researcher. Low response rates reduce the credibility and usefulness of surveys.

What can be done to address these issues? The evaluator must be sensitive to these issues and vigilant in assessing the impact of the data-gathering methods on the quality of the data. Quantum physicists remind us that measurement is not benign. Measurement changes that which is measured. This limitation never goes away, but it can be managed. Here are some strategies for managing survey data collection:

☐ *Provide some education about the ROI evaluation.* An educated respondent is often the best provider of data. An equipment manufacturer, for example, made available through their intranet a short course on ROI evaluation. People who were involved in strategic change initiatives were required to take this course before taking surveys that assessed the value of these initiatives. This approach greatly increased the value of the data and enabled more data to be collected via surveys.

☐ *When possible, conduct group administrations.* Proctoring group administrations of surveys ensures that survey data are collected in a timely way and increases response rates. If people show up to the group session, they will compete the surveys. Administering surveys in this way also allows people to ask questions as they complete sections of the questionnaire. Having their questions answered in a timely way increases the quality of the data.

☐ *Be aware of the context of surveys in the organization.* Many organizations conduct several surveys every year. Employee opinion surveys, change readiness surveys, and benefits satisfaction surveys are a few examples. Administering ROI surveys must be timed so that no overlap with these other surveys occurs. There also may be opportunities to have ROI data collection piggyback on other surveys. Some ROI data may be able to be collected through other, regularly administered surveys. One cautionary note, however, is to be aware of the historical response rates of these other surveys. If these rates are too low, these surveys should be avoided, not exploited, for the ROI analysis.

☐ *Debrief respondents on their experiences with the survey.* Understanding the impact of a survey can best be done by asking the respondents to comment on their experience. If parts of the questionnaire were confusing, they will say so. If they felt that some major sources of benefits were not being adequately captured by the questionnaire, they will say so. These comments can be extremely valuable when analyzing the data. In some cases, if it appears that enough people had a significant issue with an aspect of the survey, then secondary data collection procedures can be used to recover the missing data.

☐ *Pretest the survey materials.* Before administering a survey on a large-scale basis, conduct a mini-pilot of the survey materials. Flush out problems and issues with the questionnaire, the instructions, and other materials related to the survey. Examine the data to ensure that large-scale administration will yield the expected data in a quality and timely way.

What Is the Fastest, Easiest Way to Use Surveys to Isolate the Effects of the Initiative?

This is *the* question—the Holy Grail of ROI analysis. Let's first keep in mind that isolating the effects of a strategic change initiative is best done with multiple measures: pre-/post-initiative analysis, comparison groups, and so on. Having said this, surveys can offer a powerful and credible approach to isolate the effects of an initiative. Let's start with a questionnaire example and then turn to lessons learned.

An Example of a Questionnaire that Isolates the Effects of an Initiative

The questionnaire items illustrated in Figure 9.1 were drawn from a larger survey given to sales managers who participated in the Customer First initiative. This initiative implemented a consultative selling process based on

1. How has the company benefited from your participation in Customer First?

   _____

   _____

   _____

2. How would you categorize these benefits in terms of (please check all that apply):
   a. Increased your personal sales   _____
   b. Increased the sales of your salespeople   _____
   c. Increased your productivity   _____
   d. Increased the productivity of your salespeople   _____
   e. Reduced annualized cost of selling to customers   _____

3. For each item checked above, please answer the following:

Please use these standard values when estimating the monetary improvement.

Multiply total sales times the margin of 23%.
For productivity, multiply the number of hours times $75.

Letter Code	Estimate Monetary Improvement of Performance	Estimate % of Improvement due to Customer First	State Confidence in This Estimate (on a Percentage Basis; 0% No Confidence; 100% High Confidence)
_____	$_____	_____ %	_____ %

Based on: Daily
Weekly
Circle   Monthly
One   Quarterly
Yearly

Briefly describe the benefit: _____

_____

_____

4. How can the benefits cited above be verified by a third-party source?

   _____

   _____

   _____

(Note: Questions 3 and 4 are repeated four more times)

Figure 9.1 Example of a questionnaire that isolates the improvement of a strategic change initiative.

first understanding the customers' high-value needs and then meeting these needs with a suite of financial products and services. Managers, who were also involved in selling, were expected to increase their personal sales as well as the sales of those who reported to them. These questions have been modified to illustrate how to isolate the effects of an initiative.

Let's examine this questionnaire in detail. The first question is intended to allow the respondent to open up and state the benefits in his or her own words. The respondent may identify many benefits: some tangible, some intangible. The next two questions deal with the tangible benefits, but it is also important to capture the intangible benefits for the complete evaluation of the initiative. Also, the respondent may identify tangible benefits that do not show up in question two. In this case, a secondary analysis can be conducted to capture these additional tangible benefits.

The second question gets specific. Of all the benefits the respondent cited in the first question, what can be captured in terms of the five items noted in question 2? Listing these five items, and not other items, is based on assumptions that the researcher is making about how the business value of the initiative was expressed. To the extent that these assumptions were correct, the survey is focused and effective. If these assumptions are not correct, then the survey runs the risk of missing the mark. If benefits from the initiative really came from sources other than increases in sales and productivity or reductions in selling cost, then this survey would not capture these other benefits.

The third question is where the rubber meets the road. For each of the benefit sources checked in question 2, the respondent estimates the monetary improvement. This estimate is qualified by the percentage that the improvements resulted from the initiative and the error factor of that estimate. These are complex calculations. A brief job aid is presented in question 3 to assist in determining the monetary values. This important concept can help people make these calculations. This job aid can be expanded on to have more information or to include examples. If this course is taken, the job aid should be a separate (and facing) page in the questionnaire, or this information could be placed on a card that accompanies the survey. Many researchers voice caution in the use of examples because these examples have been shown to influence how people answer the questions. Some judgment is required here, and choosing the best course of action depends on the sophistication level of respondents. Those who are least familiar with ROI methodology would likely benefit most from some examples of completing this section of the survey.

Note that the respondent in this survey does not complete the calculations and qualify the financial benefits. In other words, the respondent estimates contribution and confidence but does not actually multiply the monetary benefits by these two percentages. This is done for a couple of reasons. First, it discourages someone from tabulating a personal financial benefit that can be compared with the benefits produced by other people. This minimizes the competitive nature of the data collection (especially important with salespeople!). The second reason is that these calculations are complex and require a calculator. Respondents would not always be accurate, and many might experience frustration in going through the calculation process. In any event, the calculations are time consuming, and time is the enemy of accurate survey completion.

The final question in this series, question 4, is very important. Experience shows that people will be more circumspect with identifying benefits when they must provide a third-party source for verification. Not all benefits, and really only a fraction of the benefits, will be verified by a third party. Generally, only the largest benefits cited will be verified. If, for example, a respondent cites an annualized cost reduction benefit of $400,000, then this would have to be verified in order to be included in the benefits. If no third-party source for this verification was identified, then the benefit would not be included in the analysis.

Lessons Learned

☐ Make the questionnaire as short as possible so that the questions are focused on the specific information needed for the ROI analysis.

☐ Use open-ended questions so that respondents can express benefits of the initiative in their own words.

☐ Present questions or items in an easy-to-read, intuitive format.

☐ Include all possible sources of value. Important sources that are left out will inevitably lower the benefits total of the initiative.

☐ Include job aids to anticipate questions and assist respondents in completing the survey in an accurate and timely way.

☐ Always ask for third-party verification. Larger benefits must be verified, and demonstrating verification of selected benefits will increase the credibility of the data.

HOW CAN RESPONSE RATES BE INCREASED?

Low response rates are the Achilles heel of surveys. The response rate is the percentage of people who complete and return the questionnaire in comparison to the total number of people who received the question-naire. Generally speaking, a 70% response rate or higher is required to establish the survey's credibility, validity, and utility for data analysis. When response rates dip much below this figure—say, in the 50% to 60% range—questions may be rightfully asked about how representa-tive the respondents are of the entire population. Why did so many people not respond to the survey? Are the nonrespondents different from respondents in some way? Did these differences in some way skew the data in one direction or another?

Lower response rates also compromise the ability of the researcher to compare the responses between subgroups. Subgroups are sets of respon-dents with particular characteristics (e.g., female executives from the western U.S. business group). As a general rule, subgroups should have at least 10 respondents to be used for comparison purposes. Any number less than 10 complicates the use of statistics, and even more important, diminishes the privacy of data for those who are in the subgroup. In no cases should data be reported for groups of fewer than five respondents.

There are many ways to increase the response rate. First and fore-most, the importance of completing the survey must be explicitly stated to the respondents, preferably by a senior leader of the organization. The timing for administering the survey is also important. Make sure that the survey does not conflict with other major corporate events or other surveys. For example, a survey that is presented during the performance appraisal process or the annual budgeting process is doomed to get lost in the shuffle. Incentives may be offered to complete the survey, although in business settings tangible incentives are not often used. Offering respondents a copy of the survey results can be an effective and accept-able incentive to increase response rates. Multiple administrations of the survey have proven to be effective to increase response rates. Generally, in business settings the first survey administration will net about a 50% to 60% response rate, the second administration will gain an additional 10% to 15%, and the third administration about 5% or less.

Survey administration generally takes about two to three weeks to complete. Each survey is numbered as it is received. During this time it is important to examine the surveys as they come in. If certain sections are not being completed or are being completed incorrectly, then the researcher can immediately take corrective actions such as sending out an additional explanatory message to the survey population. Trends may become evident as well. For example, if those surveys returned earlier tend to be more positive in the responses than those surveys returned later, it may be worth exploring whether bias has been introduced into the sample. Response rates that are much higher for one region than other regions or for one group over another group, such as females over males, may also indicate that bias has been introduced into the sample. In these cases, corrective actions may be taken by better targeting second or third administrations of the survey. It is also possible to statistically balance the data, which will reduce the effects of bias, although this measure is best left to experienced statisticians.

Response rates may also be affected by external events that happen during the survey administration. Examples could include having an organization's intranet shut down for a few days because of an invasive computer virus, severe weather, or a major news event that disrupts employees' ability to concentrate on their work. These events, if they occur, must be noted in the write-up of the survey results because they may introduce bias in the data if one group is affected more than another. A severe winter storm in a western division of a company, for example, could reduce employees' response rates below those in an eastern division. In this case, the researcher would likely give employees in the western division more time to complete and return the survey.

What Are the Essential Elements of ROI Questionnaire Construction?

Every questionnaire has an opening statement, a body of research questions, demographic questions, and a closing statement. Each of these four elements must be carefully crafted to create a quality survey that produces the intended results. In addition, most surveys will be accompanied by a cover letter to encourage employees to complete the survey. The cover letter explains the purpose of the survey, states how the results will benefit the company and employees, and highlights some general guidelines for completion. The privacy of the data collection and reporting process must be emphasized.

Opening Statement

A brief opening statement at the beginning of the survey is intended to encourage employees to complete the survey. Themes from the cover letter can be reinforced. For example, the cover letter should state the purpose for the survey, the benefits of completing the survey, and a commitment to keep the data private. This statement should be brief and to the point and with emphasis on encouraging the person to complete the survey. A privacy statement will reduce people's anxiety about their individual data being released and reviewed by others. Respondents need to know that results will be "reported in group form only and no individual names will be reported."

Research Questions

The body of research questions must be organized so that respondents can complete the survey in a timely fashion and with a mix of open-ended and close-ended questions to acquire quantitative and qualitative data. Questionnaires that take about 20 to 25 minutes to complete are optimum. Any time less than this and the researcher may not be getting all of the information required for a thorough analysis. When questionnaires take longer than 25 minutes, respondents become less likely to complete and return the survey. As a general rule of thumb, an open-ended question takes about 3 minutes to complete and a close-ended (e.g., multiple-choice) question takes about 15 seconds. When constructing a survey, researchers need to review the questionnaire and tally the time it would take a respondent to complete each question. If the aggregate time is greater than 25 minutes, consideration must be given to shortening the survey.

Open-Ended vs. Close-Ended Questions

An important consideration in constructing a survey is how best to use open-ended vs. close-ended questions. Open-ended questions require the respondent to write in his or her answer. The primary advantage of this type of question is that it produces qualitative data: Respondents express their views in their own words often providing insights into issues that the research would not know otherwise. These data provide a rich source of quotes—not attributed of course—that can be included in the final research report. These quotes often capture themes or express the opinions of groups of people in an articulate and authentic way. Open-ended questions take longer to complete, and if there are too many in the questionnaire, some respondents will be tempted to stop completing the survey. The primary disadvantage of the open-ended question is the complexity of data analysis. A technique known as content analysis can be performed, although this requires a more advanced understanding of statistical procedures.

Close-ended questions offer a menu of predetermined choices as a way of answering the question. These menus range from simple "yes/no" choices to choices of seven, ten, or more responses. The advantage of close-ended questions is the ability to gain consistent data from all respondents that can be readily analyzed. All respondents answer the same question according to predetermined choices, which enables the researcher to quickly tally and analyze the data. Of course, this requires the researcher to know what the right choices are to accurately capture respondents' viewpoints and perspectives. These types of questions can be quickly answered by the respondents, so the use of close-ended questions can increase the total amount of data that the survey can produce in contrast to the use of open-ended questions.

Reversal Questions

One disadvantage with close-ended questions is that some respondents fall into a response pattern, whereby they will routinely check off a response category without reading the question. For example, a respondent may keep answering "strongly agree" to a set of questions without actually reading the questions. A strategy to counter this tendency is to sprinkle reversal questions into the body of questions. Reversal questions are those that express the opposite position from the other questions. For example, a reversal question may express a negative outcome ("Senior management does not communicate effectively") in a body of questions that express positive outcomes ("Work teams collaborate effectively").

Scaling

Scaling opens up another dimension for close-ended questions. A scale enables measurement of one or more dimensions such as "agreement/disagreement" or "effectiveness." This allows the results from an entire category of questions to be grouped together and summarized. So, for example, a series of eight questions about senior management that all ask for an assessment of "effectiveness" can be grouped together to provide one number that represents all of the respondents' assessments of senior management effectiveness.

Scales typically consist of four to ten numerical choices and can be even or odd numbered. Larger scales provide respondents with more answer choices and can therefore increase the variation of responses. Greater response variation may be desirable in cases where the researcher wants to amplify differences among groups. For example, in Figure 9.2, scale A features a 1–10 scale that offers respondents greater opportunity to express nuances of their opinions about effectiveness than

A. Even-numbered scale assessing impact with 10 response categories

Not At All Effective									Very Effective
1	2	3	4	5	6	7	8	9	10

B. Even-numbered scale assessing effectiveness

Not At All Effective	Somewhat Effective	Effective	Very Effective
1	2	3	4

C. Odd-numbered scale with neutral choice assessing agreement/disagreement

Strongly Disagree	Disagree	Neither Agree or Disagree	Agree	Strongly Agree
1	2	3	4	5

D. Even-numbered scale forcing a choice between agreement and disagreement

Strongly Disagree	Disagree	Agree	Strongly Agree
1	2	3	4

Figure 9.2 Examples of response scales.

would scale B, which is a 1–4 scale. Even-numbered scales can be structured to make the respondent commit to one of two choices. Scale C features two choices for disagreement (1, 2), one neutral choice (3), and two choices for agreement (4, 5). The neutral choice in this scale allows respondents to not take a stand and either agree or disagree. Scale D is an even-numbered scale and forces respondents to either agree or disagree.

Demographic Questions

Including demographic questions at the end of the survey document enables the researcher to characterize survey respondents and to open further analysis opportunities. Examples of demographic questions that are typically asked in a questionnaire include company tenure, function, level or job title, and gender. Comparing the demographic profile of the respondents with the greater population shows how representative the sample of respondents is to the greater population. If, for example, the survey respondents are only 18% female, while females represent 52% of the greater population, then it could be said that the sample underrepresented females, and (without statistical adjustment) sample results cannot be generalized to the greater population.

Demographic information opens the ability to ask additional research questions that are of special interest for people. These questions explore potential interaction effects. An interaction effect is when one variable changes as a result of changes in another variable. For example, one variable, collaboration, may be stronger at lower levels in the organization than in higher levels (the other variable being organization level).

Some examples of demographic-based questions include:

- ☐ "Do senior leaders rate collaboration and teamwork higher than middle managers?"
- ☐ "Do female team members rate the diversity initiative different than male team members?"
- ☐ "Are team members with the longest tenure more or less positive about the prospects for culture change?"

The answers to questions like these can have a big impact on how change initiatives are designed and deployed. If senior leaders rate their collaboration and teamwork very low, for example, it is clear that the change initiative must place added emphasis on addressing these leadership issues.

Closing Statement

The intention of the closing statement is to thank the respondent for completing the survey. Instructions are given about how to return the completed survey, and contact information is provided in case the respondent would like to ask questions about the survey or provide additional information. It is important to give respondents options about how to return the survey. Some respondents are sensitive about the confidentiality of their data. Sending the surveys to a third-party researcher will often allay these sensitivities. Surveys that are returned to people within the organization must be done in a way that the data cannot be linked to particular individuals. It is commonplace now to complete and return surveys via intranets or e-mail. Respondents must be able to return their surveys electronically without their data being associated with their e-mail addresses or other identity markers. Some respondents will remain suspicious, however, so a surface mail address should also be provided.

CHAPTER 10

ROI on the Fly: Evaluating an Initiative After It Has Been Deployed

WHAT TO DO WHEN YOUR CEO ASKS: "WHAT HAVE YOU DONE FOR ME LATELY?"

This chapter was originally entitled: "OK, I have ignored everything in this book, I don't even want to do evaluation, but my CEO asked me how my recently completed OD initiative added value to the business, so now what do I do?" Although this title is too long, the sentiment is real, so let's take this issue head-on. First, don't panic. Panic is an unbridled expression of emotion that will make many CEOs nervous. A CEO who asks this question about value wants reassurance, not a nervous breakdown. Next, be prepared to enter the world of ROI on the fly.

"ROI on the fly" refers to embracing the spirit of this book, while adapting the letter of this book to the realities of a less-is-more world. A post-initiative evaluation is usually undertaken several weeks or even months after deployment has been completed. A big investment was made in the initiative and the ROI is not immediately obvious. The CEO's curiosity gets the better of him or her, and then an evaluation is called for to determine what value the change initiative added to the organization and how this value can be increased or leveraged in the future.

The major challenge with post-initiative evaluations is that the evaluation data must be reconstructed. Table 10.1 shows what a barebones evaluation would look like in this case. The intention here is to reconstruct the data from the initiative as much as possible, filling in the blanks as needed.

Table 10.1 ROI on the Fly Checklist

Phase	Process	Outcomes
Diagnosis	Reconstruct the business and initiative objectives. Work with the client to make a reasonable linkage	Business and initiative objectives
	Define the performance gap	Business rationale for the initiative
Design	Develop reasonable evaluation objectives	Evaluation objectives
Develop	Decide on how best to evaluate the initiative	Evaluation plan
	Develop data collection instruments	Data collection instruments
Deploy	Collect data on who participated in the initiative or who was affected by the initiative	List of participants in the target population
	Communicate your intentions to do the evaluation	Key messages
	Conduct the evaluation	Data set
Reflect	Analyze the results	Data analysis write-up
	Report the findings and conclusions	ROI and recommendations

Diagnosis

One of the first challenges confronting the ROI on the fly process is that the quality of the diagnosis may have been shortchanged. The performance gap may not have been well defined, and the initiative objective may not have been linked to the organization goals. If this is the case, these areas will have to be reconstructed. A business case, if one was done, can be a great place to start. First, based on available data, make the best guess you can about the performance gap. Begin with the outcomes of the initiative: How did the initiative improve performance? If performance improvements are not obvious, rely on the expected outcomes of the initiative to suggest performance improvement areas. Translate these outcomes into a performance statement. Include in this statement the level of performance before the initiative was launched and what level of performance is expected. This approach yields the performance gap.

Next, create initiative objectives that, if achieved, would close the per-formance gap. At the very least, there were likely stated intentions for how the initiative would improve the business. Build on these intentions to state a reasonable connection from the initiative to the needed per-formance improvements. Write one or more initiative objectives (along the lines suggested in Chapter 3) that formally link initiative outcomes with desired performance improvements.

Now come the business goals. Map the initiative objectives to one or more of the top business goals. Make these linkages as explicit as pos-sible. The CEO's question about value will ultimately come down to the impact that the initiative had on these business goals. In this way, the line-of-sight linkage described in Chapter 3 can be reconstructed. This reconstruction process is not perfect, so work with the business leaders to make reasonable judgment calls.

Design

Given that we are doing an evaluation after the fact, the initiative design has been set in stone. All that can be done at this point is to develop reasonable evaluation objectives that link to the initiative objectives. A litmus test for these objectives is to ask if meeting these objectives could reasonably close the performance gap. If so, then the barebones logic of the line-of-sight linkage has been established from business goal to initiative objective to evaluation objective. If a case cannot be made that meeting these evaluation objectives would close the performance gap, then it's back to the drawing board to rewrite these objectives. Some connection between performance and the evaluation, however tenuous, must be made. Otherwise, the outcome of the evaluation, which is guided by these objectives, will have little bearing on the measured per-formance. Without demonstrated performance improvements, very little can be said about the impact of the initiative on business goals. There is little point in proceeding with an evaluation that people know in advance will not answer the CEO's question about value to the business.

Develop

People conducting a post-initiative evaluation have few options avail-able to them to isolate effects of the initiative. The time to utilize pilots, for example, has long since gone. Other comparison groups are likely no longer in consideration. Despite this limitation, the client and evalu-ator must decide how best to evaluate the initiative to isolate its effect on organization performance (however this has been defined) and translate these effects to monetary terms.

Let the evaluation objectives be your guide. Post-initiative evaluation activities focus directly on collecting data for these evaluation objectives. These activities include a follow-up questionnaire regarding application of the initiative, a focus group of people involved in the deployment, or a survey of customers to determine how the initiative affected them. Archival data can also be accessed (e.g., production data, quality performance data, and other surveys that were conducted during the initiative). An evaluation plan is developed that features one or more, and typically several, of these activities. Then data collection tools and instruments are developed for the evaluation activities included in the plan. All of these data collection activities boil down to answering the fundamental question discussed in Chapter 5: How can the effects of the initiative be isolated from all other influencing factors? The primary difference here is that Chapter 5 shows how to proactively answer this question, whereas with ROI on the fly it is an after-the-fact forensic process.

Deploy

This forensic journey of evaluation begins by rounding up a list of suspects or, in this case, participants. Records from the deployment can reveal who participated in the initiative, what organizational areas or regions were involved and when, and which organization units were affected by the initiative. Leaders who were involved in the initiative can also be interviewed to identify participants. This list of participants will be used to draw the names of people who will complete the surveys or participate in the focus groups that will provide critical evaluation data. The quality of these data, and the willingness of the people to participate in providing the data, depends largely on how well prepared these people are to be a part of the evaluation. Potential participants must understand the reason for the evaluation and the valuable role they are expected to play. Some people may be reluctant to participate because the initiative is a distant memory for them and they doubt that they can provide reliable data. Key messages, often developed in the form of talking points, are developed and communicated to potential participants to enlist their support and to reassure them that they have valuable knowledge and insights into the effects of the initiative.

Everyone in the organization, regardless of whether they participate in the evaluation, needs to know why this evaluation is being conducted and what will be done with the data. If people do not hear from the leadership why the initiative is being evaluated, they will fill in the information void with their own ideas. These ideas can grow and mingle to form juicy rumors. These rumors can take on a life of their own ("The CEO is questioning the value of the initiative and heads may roll!") and can greatly compromise the quality of an evaluation ("They are looking for scapegoats, so watch your back!"). It is in everyone's best interest to clearly and honestly state why the evaluation is being conducted and how the results will be used (and not used).

This explanation paves the way for the evaluation to be conducted. Surveys are administered, focus groups are conducted, and key initiative participants are interviewed. All data are organized to address the evaluation objectives and determine the value of the initiative to the business.

Reflect

The evaluation brings all data together to tell a story about the strategic impact of the initiative. This story features tangible and qualitative data. Tangible, monetary benefits of the program are identified, the effects of the initiative are isolated, initiative costs are tabulated, and the ROI is calculated, as detailed in Chapter 7. Post initiative evaluation is often an excellent time to gather qualitative data. People have had the time to more deeply reflect on their experiences and to draw insights from these experiences. These insights may point to significant sources of intangible value and suggest future initiatives.

A brief, 5- to 10-page report of the findings is prepared for the client that basically follows the format provided in Chapter 7. ROIs and BCRs are featured in the context of providing monetary and intangible benefits of the initiative. The CEO's original question can finally be answered. Recommendations are made about how to sustain the gains and leverage the learnings more broadly in the organization.

Let's see how the ROI on the fly process really works through the following case study.

CASE STUDY: CONDUCTING A POST-INITIATIVE ANALYSIS AT POWER SYSTEMS

Background

In 2001, 14 dealers from Latin America–based Power Systems (fictitious name) had their sales representatives participate in a comprehensive program that was intended to increase yearly revenue by improving sales performance. Sales did increase steadily throughout the year, but why?

By mid-2002, business leaders wanted to know the contribution that the performance improvement initiative made on increased sales. Evaluation, including ROI, was conducted to determine the financial and intangible business benefits of the performance improvement program for both the manufacturer and the dealers who participated in this effort.

Diagnosis

1. *Reconstruct the business and initiative objectives.* This was fairly straightforward, given that the intention of the initiative was to increase sales; however, specific targets were not set for the initiative. It was generally assumed that the new sales process and more lucrative incentives would drive up sales. Sales targets were set higher (stretch goals) for each of the dealerships and varied according to local market conditions and other factors.

2. *Define the performance gap.* The performance gap was operationally defined as the difference between sales in 2000 and the stretch sales goals in 2001. It was decided that sales data for all dealers would be combined for the analysis. The combined performance for these dealers indicated that they met their stretch goals, so this performance gap was closed. The question turned to how much of this performance improvement resulted from the initiative.

Design

3. *Develop reasonable evaluation objectives.* The focus of this evaluation was clear, especially given the short timeframe to conduct the evaluation: How much of the increase in sales could be attributed to the performance improvement initiative? Business leaders did throw in one curveball to the evaluation. They felt that loyal customers would buy from their company no matter what, so they wanted these sales taken out of the ROI equation. This consideration refined the evaluation objective somewhat, so everyone involved in the evaluation settled on the following objective: Increase in sales attributable to the initiative from new customers and "win-back" (e.g., former) customers in 2001 from 2000 levels for the 14 dealerships.

Develop

4. *Decide how best to evaluate the initiative.* In the interest of speed, ROI analysis for the sales performance improvement program

relied on existing data. The evaluator spent three days at the company headquarters and collected the following data:

☐ Investment (cost) levels for the initiative for both manufacturers and dealers. It was learned that the manufacturer partially subsidized the cost of the initiative for its dealers.

☐ Dealer net revenue dollars for 2000 and 2001 of the 14 participating dealers according to three sales classifications:

1. *Win-back revenue.* Former customers who purchased engine products from competitors and then in 2001 once again became Power Systems customers. Gaining this revenue required the highest level of sales capability as developed by the initiative.

2. *New customer revenue.* First-time customers in 2001. Gaining this revenue required a higher level of sales capability. This was less challenging than winning back former customers and easier than selling to loyal customers.

3. *Loyal customers.* Customers who continued to purchase engine products in 2001. Gaining this revenue required a high level of sales capability, but of the three categories, was the easiest to accomplish.

☐ Surveys and interview data that indicated how people applied what they gained from the initiative and how effectively they followed the new sales process.

5. *Develop data collection instruments.* It was decided that the best way to isolate the effects of the initiative was through expert estimation. Natural comparison groups did not present themselves as an option. All dealerships participated, and within the dealerships participation was mandatory. A discussion protocol was developed for a focus group format. The purpose of the focus group was to isolate the effects of the initiative.

Deploy

6. *Collect data on who participated in the initiative or who was affected by the initiative.* Data on the sales performance of individual participants for the 14 dealerships were not readily available. So, in the interest of speed, these data were not collected.

7. *Communicate your intentions to do the evaluation.* Key messages were developed to explain to the dealerships why this study was being conducted. For the most part, people were curious about

the outcome of the study and that the effects of the initiative could be isolated and converted to monetary value. Everyone was cooperative.

8. *Conduct the evaluation.* Given that this evaluation was conducted one year after the initiative was deployed, the options to isolate the effects of the initiative were somewhat limited. Two options presented themselves: documenting pre-/post-initiative changes in net revenue, and gaining expert estimates of revenue changes resulting from the initiative.

☐ *Pre-/post-initiative changes in net revenue.* The increase in dealer net revenue from 2000 to 2001 was $19.6 million. The loyal customer dealer net revenue increase of $2.8 million was excluded from cost benefits because a portion of that increase would likely have happened without the initiative. Dealer net revenue increase of $19.6 million was classified as coming from win-back customers and new customers. Although these benefits were partly the result of the performance improvement initiative, further isolation of program effects was required.

☐ *Expert estimates to isolate effects.* Experts were drawn from throughout the company to isolate the effects of the initiative. These experts included salespeople, sales managers, and program managers. A focus group was assembled on a conference call and facilitated by the evaluator. The purpose of the study was explained and a discussion protocol followed that closely mirrors the series of questions presented in Table 9.1. Other major influencing factors were identified, and the effects of these factors were isolated. Collectively, these people estimated the isolation factor of the initiative to be 24.4% (includes contribution and confidence factors).

Reflect

9. *Analyze the results.* The qualified benefits were calculated as follows:

Qualified benefits = $19.6 million × 24.4% isolation factor

= $4.8 million

Total program costs for both participant groups were determined to be:

Manufacturer $460,000
Dealers $208,460

The ROI was calculated as follows:

$$ROI = (Benefits - Cost) \div Cost) \times 100:$$

ROI for Manufacturer

$4.8 million $\times$ 12% margin = $576,000

$ROI = ($567,000 - $460,000) \div $460,000) \times 100 = 25\%$

ROI for Dealers

Calculating the ROI for the dealers required an additional step. Revenue incremental from engine sales had to be determined. The incremental revenue refers to the value-added revenue that comes after the engine sale. For example, service level agreements and maintenance contracts with much higher margins would be sold to the customers. Incremental revenue added 150% to the sale of the engines.

$4.8 million $\times$ 150% incremental revenue = $7.2 million

$7.2 million $\times$ 12% margin = $1.2 million

$ROI = ($1,200,000 - $208,460) \div $208,460) \times 100 = 476\%$

Data from the surveys and questionnaires that were administered during deployment of the initiative were examined. Many stories were pulled from the data, which helped illustrate how the sales initiative contributed to achieving the sales performance goals. These qualitative data added credibility to the final analysis.

10. *Report the findings.* The findings clearly showed that the sales performance improvement initiative offered dealers a proven approach to increase net revenue. The manufacturer was able to offer this program to dealers at cost (25% ROI), enabling dealers to realize a significant return on their investment (467% ROI). Recommendations were made about how to build on this initiative to accelerate sales growth. These recommendations included revamping some sales support processes and reinforcing the leaders' role in sustaining the gains.

FREQUENTLY ASKED QUESTIONS

This brief case study shows how the evaluation process can be adapted to a situation but not compromised in the process. Challenges arose when evaluation process steps were not followed. These leave blank holes in the evaluation, which in some cases were quite large holes to fill. After all, ROI on the fly is a forensic process, so it is expected that there will be some gaps. Some frequently asked questions about closing these gaps include the following:

Q: What happens when the initiative objectives do not clearly link to the business goals?

A: This happens more often than one might think or expect. In many cases, these links are simply assumed. For example, the sales improvement initiative was assumed to increase sales. Logically, this seemed reasonable and the evaluation eventually bore out this assumption; however, one can only speculate how much more effective the initiative would have been if specific targets had been set or if the initiative had been originally designed to get at the heart of the performance gap.

As an evaluator in this situation, the simple answer is to work directly with the client so that these decisions are made to everyone's mutual satisfaction. If no apparent link exists between the initiative objectives and the business goals, strong consideration should be given to not doing the evaluation. The initiative can still be evaluated, but to what end? The initiative may have generated increases in productivity, but if productivity is not a key strategic business issue, then the evaluation results will be of little strategic interest. The bigger question for the client is how this situation could have happened in the first place. In other words, how could a major initiative have been launched and completed with so little apparent consideration given to its true strategic impact?

Q: How can meaningful estimation data be collected only after the deployment?

A: Memory fades, to be sure, and as time goes on, many people tend to remember more of the positives than the negatives. There is no hard-and-fast time limit after an initiative has been deployed for when estimation data can no longer be gathered. It really boils down to a matter of judgment between the client and the evaluator. In the preceding example, the timing was actually pretty good. Enough time had elapsed from deployment of the initiative so that real increases in sales volume could be seen. Also, this time lapse provided the people making the estimates with perspectives on other potential influences on sales performance.

In part, the answer to this question on timing depends on what is being estimated. Salespeople are immediately able to utilize the performance initiative to work with customers. But how long is the sales cycle? In other words, if it takes 10 months to make a sale once the potential customer is contacted, then estimating the impact of the initiative on sales would have to be pushed out accordingly. Improvements in warranty costs, to take an extreme case, will likely not show up for two or even three years. Expert estimation is out of the question for warranty costs, even if everyone is taking a daily dose of gingko biloba to enhance memory. Like so much of the evaluation process, judgment and common sense are the best guides.

Q: What can be done when the initiative team members get defensive about conducting this kind of evaluation?

A: It's hard not to be defensive when the CEO taps you on the shoulder and asks you how you are creating value for the business. Typically, a CEO who is asking this question is already in the process of making up his or her mind. If the CEO already sees how the initiative added value, he or she likely wouldn't ask the question. Often, how people react to this question will greatly influence how well the CEO will receive the answer. People who react defensively raise other people's defenses as well. People get caught in a trap about defending and not taking the high ground of understanding. It's best to view the CEO's question in a positive light and take it at face value. Recognize that the CEO has asked to be educated about the strategic value of an initiative. Treat this as a teachable moment for him or her and invest the time in providing a quality and insightful answer. If taken in the right light, this can be a time to shine for the change practitioner.

SECTION THREE

Case Studies

This section presents three case studies that are at the cutting edge of strategic change valuation. The benefits of these three strategic change initiatives, that heretofore have been relegated to be intangible, are demonstrated to show monetary value to the business. These case studies are meant to bring the strategic change valuation process to life, illustrated with real-world examples. The first case study deals with executive coaching. A comprehensive study is conducted that evaluates coaching along the lines of the five levels of analysis. The ROI shows that coaching produced more than a 700% ROI for the business. Recommendations are made about how to increase the value of coaching for the business. The second case study deals with demonstrating an ROI for aligning the capabilities of the organization to a newly created strategy. The organization capability alignment process produced a 1000% ROI. The third case study addresses the topic of knowledge management. This is one of the hottest areas in strategic change, and there is a great deal of interest in learning about how knowledge management creates tangible value for the business. This study shows how knowledge management produced ROIs of more than 400% and discusses ways to increase the business value of knowledge management. All three of these case studies show how to tame the intangibles by demonstrating the tangible, monetary benefits that these strategic change initiatives produced.

CHAPTER 11

Executive Coaching: The ROI of Building Leadership One Executive at a Time

INTRODUCTION

This *Fortune 500* company was committed to developing its leadership capability in order to support the achievement of its business strategy: achieving and maintaining leadership in its three major markets. An innovative leadership development effort was launched that was expected to accelerate the development of next-generation leaders. Participants were drawn mostly from a group of emerging leaders with a high potential for professional growth who came from many different business units and functional areas throughout North America. Leadership development activities included group mentoring, individual assessments and development planning, a leadership workshop, work on strategic business projects, and coaching.

Coaching was a key enabler for this approach to leadership development because participants could work privately and individually with their coaches to develop specific leadership competencies. The company contracted with a coaching company to provide coaching to leadership development participants. This coaching was started in Spring 2000 and was completed by Spring 2001.

The company's human resources professionals wanted to make sure that the investment in leadership development was made with maximum business benefit. Although leadership development participants spoke very highly of their experience with coaching, it was decided to conduct a formal assessment of the effectiveness and business impact of coaching. The results from this study would be used to answer the following two questions:

1. How did coaching add value for the company and specifically what was the business impact of coaching?
2. How could the company best leverage coaching in the future?

DATA COLLECTION PROCEDURES

It was decided that the best way to isolate and capture the effects of coaching on the business would be through a survey. This survey had two parts. Part 1 was completed electronically via e-mail and examined clients' initial reaction to coaching, what they learned, how they applied what they learned, and captured an initial assessment of business impact. Part 2 was conducted over the telephone with each respondent and probed potential monetary benefits due directly to the coaching. The advantages of this approach included being able to understand the unique nature of each client's experience with coaching, how this experience translated into business benefits, and being able to gather these data in a consistent and timely fashion.

This study focused on five levels of data analysis and included intangible benefits:

☐ *Level 1: Initial reaction of the clients to their coaching.* How the coach and the client initially built their relationship, established rapport, and set meaningful objectives for the coaching process.
☐ *Level 2: What clients learned from coaching.* This demonstrated the extent to which the clients gained the knowledge and insights they needed to make meaningful enhancements to their performance.
☐ *Level 3: How clients applied what they learned.* The more frequently and more broadly clients applied what they learned, the greater the likelihood they had in producing a positive impact on the business.
☐ *Level 4: The business impact of coaching.* This showed how the changes that the clients made as a result of their coaching created value for the business.
☐ *Level 5: Return on investment.* It was important to know not only the total monetary benefits of coaching, but also how this total compared to the total program cost.
☐ *Intangible benefits.* Not all benefits can be documented in financial terms. These benefits, such as customer satisfaction, can be

valuable in other ways, so it was important to capture these additional benefits.

The target population for the study was 43 participants drawn from the Eastern United States and Mexico. These participants represented a cross-section of the company's business and included those in sales, operations, technology, finance, and marketing. All participants had been identified as high potential leaders and on the fast track to become senior executives.

Profile of the Respondents and Initiation of Coaching

A total of 30 coaching clients participated in the survey for a 70% response rate. More than one-third of the respondents (37%) had direct customer contact as part of their job responsibilities, and 43% had direct reports. A few indicated that they performed mostly as project managers and would lead virtual teams in projects. Most reported titles as being a director or manager. The average tenure was 6 years, with a range of 2 to 17 years with the company. Eleven (37%) of the respondents were female.

Representatives from human resources and the coaching company met to review the development needs of the participants and the backgrounds of the coaches. This review enabled these representatives to make the most appropriate matches of coach to client. Clients were able to request a change of coaches if they desired and coaching was provided only to those people who requested it.

An introduction session was scheduled for participants to learn about coaching and to meet their coaches in person. This day-long, voluntary session was well received, but there was less than full attendance by the clients. Coaching was initiated immediately after the introductory session and conducted mostly over the telephone. Coaching sessions were generally 45 minutes in duration with each client receiving 12 to 15 sessions over a five month period. Coaches had access to their clients' 360-degree feedback results and other assessment materials to provide additional developmental focus for the coaching.

Level 1: Initial Reaction of the Clients to Their Coaching

One third (33%) of the respondents were initially skeptical that coaching was going to work for them (Figure 11.1). Many reported that they did not initially understand what coaching was or how it was going to

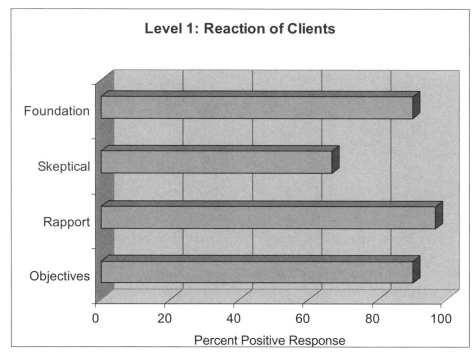

Figure 11.1 Level 1 data: The initial reaction to coaching.

help them. These issues, however, were apparently readily dealt with given the very high ratings that the clients gave the initial two or three coaching sessions. According to the clients, objectives were set (90% reported favorably), rapport was established (97%), and these initial sessions provided a strong foundation for the coaching (90%).

LEVEL 2: WHAT CLIENTS LEARNED FROM COACHING

Almost all of the respondents (97%) gained critical insights into personal changes required for them to become more effective (Figure 11.2). For most clients (93%), this included realizing how to improve communication and collaboration skills. Better understanding on how to work with peers to accomplish business objectives was cited by 83% of the respondents. Gaining greater understanding of personal impact on others (77%) and finding new ways to look at business situations (77%) were also cited as valuable skills. Overall, almost three-quarters (73%) of the clients learned how to be more effective as a leader.

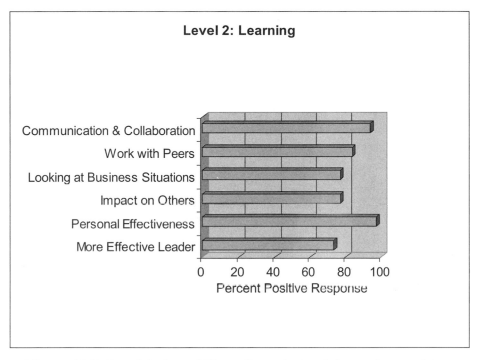

Figure 11.2 Level 2 data: What clients learned from the coaching.

Coaching sessions were characterized by the clients as rich learning conversations that fostered self-examination. Clients cited the relative safety of the coaching relationship to explore how to handle business situations. Having the coaches come from outside the company was considered a benefit. Many clients cited that the coaching enabled them to more rapidly develop as leaders, and in some cases, to develop differently as leaders. As a result of coaching, leadership styles were reported to be more inclusive of others' needs, less defensive, more supportive, and more focused on top priorities. Many clients reported planning better for approaching situations, being more open to new ideas and alternative solutions, and, for those with customer contact, being more effective with customer interactions.

LEVEL 3: HOW CLIENTS APPLIED WHAT THEY LEARNED

Seven of ten (70%) clients were better able to handle real-life business situations as a result of the coaching they received (Figure 11.3). Given

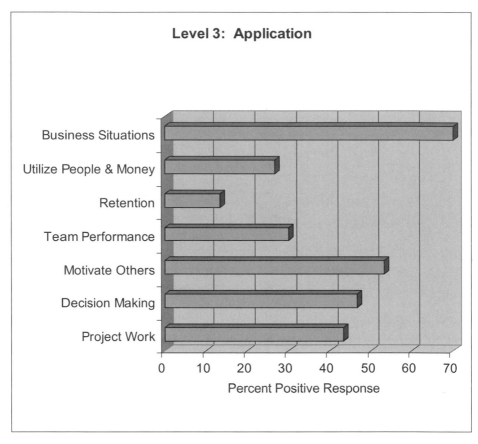

Figure 11.3 Level 3 data: Application of coaching to work.

the unique nature of each coaching relationship, the particular business situations that were addressed would naturally vary from client to client. Most (70%) were able to apply what they learned during coaching to positively influence a business situation. More than half of the clients (53%) were better able to motivate others to accomplish business objectives. At least four of ten clients improved the quality and/or speed of decision making (47%) and made work on business projects more effective (43%). About one-quarter of the clients applied their learning from coaching to improve team performance (30%) and to better utilize people and money (27%). Only 13% of the clients reported increasing retention of team members who reported to them.

Eleven of the clients cited additional applications for their coaching. These included engaging others more effectively, dealing with downsizing and restructuring, navigating internal politics, defining objectives and creating action plans to achieve these objectives, and better managing a work/life balance.

LEVEL 4: THE BUSINESS IMPACT OF COACHING

Three-quarters (77%) of the respondents indicated that coaching had a significant or very significant impact on at least one of nine business impact areas. In-depth discussions were conducted over the telephone with each respondent. More than half of the respondents (60%) were able to identify specific financial benefits that came as a result of their coaching. Table 11.1 presents each of the nine business impact areas, shows the percentage of respondents who cited each business impact area as being significantly affected by coaching, shows the percentage of respondents who cited financial benefits, and totals the monetary benefits for each business impact area. The comments section provides additional information about the benefits documented by the participants. These monetary benefits reported by the respondents. Rather, these benefits have been isolated as directly due to coaching. The next section, Procedures for Calculating Monetary Benefits, describes the isolation in more detail.

Overall, productivity (60%) and employee satisfaction (53%) were cited as the areas most significantly affected by the coaching. Respondents defined productivity in this context mostly as relating to their personal or workgroup productivity. Half (50%) of the respondents documented $277,526 in annualized productivity benefits. Employee satisfaction was viewed in terms of the respondents being personally more satisfied as a result of the coaching, as well as being able to increase the satisfaction of their team members. The respondents could not quantify this benefit in financial terms. This, then, was a significant source of intangible benefits.

Work output (30%) and work quality (40%) were cited by respondents as being significantly affected by coaching. These two areas were tightly linked in the minds of the respondents. Both areas related to the outcomes of actions taken by the respondents, and in some cases their work teams, which produced tangible financial benefits. Twenty percent of the respondents identified $947,208 in benefits as a result of increased work output. Many respondents reported improvements in work quality, but they were not able to quantify these improvements in terms of dollar benefits. Work quality improvements was considered to be an intangible benefit of the coaching.

Table 11.1 Summary of Business Impact

Business Impact Area	% Citing Significant Impact	% Identifying $ Benefits	$ Benefits	Comments
Work output	30	20	947,208	Benefits generated as a result of higher output of self or team through enhanced decision making, collaboration, and accelerated achievement of objectives.
Work quality	40	0	0	It was not possible to quantify these benefits and so, while substantial, these benefits will be considered intangible.
Productivity	60	50	277,526	Personal and/or team efficiency benefits expressed in terms of hours saved per week, at $75 per hour, and 48 weeks per year.
Cost control	3	3	85,200	Reduction in sales, general, and administrative expenses.
Product development cycle time	10	0	0	Very few respondents were involved in managing product development.
Employee retention	27	13	660,000	Four team members said that they would have left the company if it were not for the coaching. Three other team members said

Benefit category				Comments
Employee satisfaction	53	0		that coaching significantly influenced their staying with the company, but these three were not included in the benefits calculation. Two respondents mentioned retaining over 20 of their team members, but these benefits were not included either.
Customer satisfaction	33	0		This benefit was the second most cited of all benefit categories, but it was not possible to quantify this benefit in financial terms. This is another significant source of intangible benefits.
Sales volume	10	10	311,200	Most respondents who had customer contact indicated that customer satisfaction likely increased as a result of their changed behavior (because of coaching). This benefit was not directly measured and is considered an intangible benefit.
				Benefits are net revenue to the company (not total sales increase) based on 25% margins.
Total $ benefits			$2,281,134	

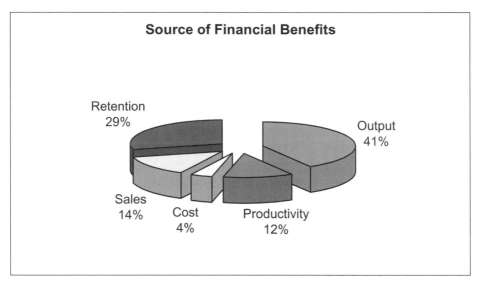

Figure 11.4 Sources of financial benefits of coaching.

Customer satisfaction (33%) and sales volume increases (10%) were cited as being affected by coaching. This translated into $311,200 of increased net revenue to the business that was identified by two respondents. A cost control (3%) reduction produced $85,200 in annualized benefits. Reducing product development cycle time (10%) was not significantly affected by coaching and yielded no measurable financial benefits.

Figure 11.4 shows the five major sources of financial benefits gained from coaching. Financial benefits gained from improvements in work output constituted 41% of the total financial benefit pie of $2,281,134. Retention was the next greatest source of financial benefit, with 29% of the total. Increased sales contributed 14%, productivity gains contributed 12%, and the cost reduction measure contributed 4% of the total financial benefit.

Respondents who had direct customer contact or who managed direct reports as part of their work responsibilities reported proportionally greater financial benefits. Respondents who directly worked with external customers (37%) produced 55% of the total financial benefits. In other words, these respondents produced, on average, $114,267 in benefits. $53,905 in benefits for those respondents who did not have direct customer contact. Respondents who had direct reports (43%) produced

68% of the benefits, or on average, produced $119,465 in benefits $42,829 in benefits for those respondents who did not have direct reports. Overall, the 30 respondents produced, on average, $76,038 in benefits. Taking the total financial benefits of $2,281,134 and dividing this total by the number of clients in the entire population (43) results in an average of $53,050.

PROCEDURES FOR CALCULATING MONETARY BENEFITS ISOLATING THE EFFECTS OF COACHING

Individual discussions with each respondent were conducted to document the monetary benefits of coaching. The researcher reviewed part 1 of the survey, the written questionnaire, to review where the respondent thought coaching had a significant impact or very significant impact on key business measurement areas. All written comments by the respondent were reviewed to better understand the work context for these potential business benefit areas. The researcher conducted a 20-minute telephone discussion with each respondent to probe how coaching may have contributed to generating financial benefits. Specific examples were documented about how coaching led directly to significant changes in behavior and how these behavior changes impacted one or more business areas. In these cases, respondents estimated the monetary impact on the business. Respondents who reported monetary benefits were then asked to estimate the percentage of this benefit (0% to 100%) that was directly attributable to coaching (isolation). These estimates averaged 75%. Respondents were then asked to say how confident they were in this estimate, from 0% to 100% confident (error). On average, respondents were 69% confident in their estimations. The monetary benefit was then multiplied by both of these percentages. All qualified (isolated) benefits were then tallied and are presented in Table 11.1.

STANDARD VALUES

Standard values were used in the calculation of monetary benefits. The human resources department provided a standard value of the average hour of a study participant to be worth $75. As a matter of procedure, the lower estimate from respondents was always used. If a respondent estimated a productivity savings of three to four hours per week, for example, the researcher would take the lower figure, three hours, for the calculation. In annualizing the benefit, the researcher would multiply the value by 48 weeks, rather than 52 weeks, to account for vacation time.

A recent study by human resources showed that the fully loaded cost per turnover of their top talent group (from which the respondents were drawn) was $330,000. This standard value includes costs of recruiting, training, lost productivity, and opportunity costs. For the purposes of this study and to be extra conservative, this standard value was cut in half to $165,000, and then this reduced value was used to calculate the retention benefits. Only the retention of the leadership participants was included in the benefits. The reported retention of the participant's direct reports was not included in the benefits total.

Respondents who were involved in sales to customers reported margins of the company's products and services to be in the range of 25% to 45%. The lowest figure, 25%, was always used to estimate financial benefits of coaching. Net sales, and not total sales, were used in the benefit calculations. Cost of money was estimated to be 10%.

Examples of Calculating Monetary Benefits

Two examples will help further clarify how monetary benefits were calculated. In the first example, a respondent reported gains in personal productivity. The coaching, she said, helped her focus on what was really important for the business (and not the "urgent but not high priority" items). She reported examples of getting more done in a shorter period and leading meetings that accomplished the agenda more quickly. She estimated three to five hours per week saved at a minimum. These savings were 80% attributed to the coaching she received, and she was 75% confident in this estimate. Benefits were calculated as follows:

3 hours @ $75 = $225 per week × 48 weeks = $10,800 per year

This value of $10,800 was then multiplied by 80% (coaching) and 75% (confidence) to yield $6,480. The value of $6,480 was entered as a productivity gain and financial benefit.

In the second example, a sales account manager indicated that coaching helped him to better handle customer sales situations, and that this ability has led to more sales. He approached customers with increased focus and was more articulate in presenting solutions to customers. He indicated that of a total of $6.8 million sales per year, at least 10% of these sales was attributable to the coaching he received. He attributed 60% of this benefit directly to coaching and was 60% confident in this estimate. Benefits were calculated as follows:

$$\$6.8 \text{ million} \times 10\% = \$680,000 \times 25\% \text{ margin} = \$170,000$$

$$\$170,000 \times 60\% \text{ due to coaching} = \$102,000 \times 60\%$$
$$\text{confidence factor} = \$61,200$$

This value of $61,200 was then entered as a benefit gain under sales.

LEVEL 5: RETURN ON INVESTMENT

Total program costs were tabulated to be $257,000. This investment includes professional fees of the coaches, evaluation costs, time the clients spent being coached, administration, travel, and other incidental expenses. It should be noted that the costs of the entire program for 43 clients were included, whereas the benefits were captured only from the 30 survey respondents. In other words, the financial benefits from the 30 respondents were spread across the costs generated by 43 coaching clients.

Coaching produced a return of investment of 788% for the company. This was calculated by:

$$\text{ROI} = ((\$\text{Benefits} - \text{Program Costs}) \div \text{Program Costs}) \times 100$$
$$\text{ROI} = ((\$2,281,134 - \$257,000) \div \$257,000) \times 100 = 788\%$$

SUMMARY OF INTANGIBLE BENEFITS

Three-quarters (77%) of the respondents thought highly enough of their coaching experience to recommend coaching to others in the company. In reviewing their written responses to explain their recommendation, almost two-thirds (63%) of the respondents reported that their coaching accelerated personal development, improved team performance, or helped them deal with downsizing and reorganizations. These benefits, while intangible, no doubt contributed positively to the business. Those who recommended coaching stressed that, in order to get the most out of coaching, it was important to be open to self-reflection, to look at situations differently, and to try new approaches to address issues. Those who would not recommend coaching complained that the process was too open-ended, not goal oriented, and that no answers were given by the coaches. Coaching was seen by this latter group as only being effective in dealing with specific situations.

Many other benefits cited in this study, while not producing a tangible financial return, did create meaningful value for the company. Significant improvements were made in both employee and customer satisfaction; decision making was improved; interpersonal relationships and collaboration were enhanced. The clients developed skills in sizing up situations and being more effective in motivating people and leading teams. Leadership skills were strengthened at a time when the company needed these skills the most. Coaching provided a key group of emerging leaders with tools and ideas about how to best handle a series of organization restructurings. It cannot be underestimated how important these tools and ideas were to effectively managing these organizational changes and keeping people motivated and focused on the business.

RECOMMENDATIONS FOR LEVERAGING COACHING

The results from this study indicate that there are seven practices for successful coaching engagements. Following these practices will ensure that maximum business value will be gained from coaching:

1. *Provide coaching with strong organizational support.* This takes two forms. First, company leaders need to stay the course and support the coaching process. The company deserves a great deal of credit for maintaining its support of coaching in the face of challenging business conditions. Second, coaching should be conducted in the context of other developmental activities. Placing coaching in the context of broader development efforts enabled participants and coaches to draw upon competency models, assessments, and learnings from mentoring and workshops to enrich the coaching experiences.

2. *Offer clients the ability to choose coaches.* Clients must be allowed to opt into the coaching relationship and choose their coaches. The selection process would be benefited by the clients having access to information about the coaches, including biographies, education, coaching credentials, functional expertise, industry experience, and other background information. Ideally, clients would be able to conduct interviews (at least over the telephone).

Whenever possible, face-to-face meetings to make the selection decision should be offered.

3. *Ensure that coaches are grounded in the company's business and culture.* Coaching is provided to clients in a business context, and the more the coaches understand this context, the more effective their coaching will be in terms of producing business results. Client company representatives should meet with the coaches at the beginning of the engagement and share the business strategy, top business priorities, and other information relevant to understanding the business. If specific business results or an ROI are expected, the coaches need to understand these expectations.

4. *Prepare clients in advance for coaching.* Clients need to understand what to expect from coaching and what their responsibilities are for making the coaching successful. Coaches should conduct an extended face-to-face induction session with each of their clients to accelerate development of the relationship. Trust is the foundation of the coaching relationship. Those clients who did have a face-to-face induction session reported that this session accelerated trust building. Many of the clients who did not attend the introduction session voiced regret and wished that they had attended.

5. *Allow each coaching relationship to follow its own path.* An important reason for the effectiveness of coaching is its strong client-driven approach to development. Coaches need wide latitude to work with the whole person and help each client be more effective as a person, as well as to be more effective as a business leader. Many clients in this study reported, for example, gaining a better work/life balance that enhanced their effectiveness in their business roles. Coaching is an effective integrator of learning and helped most clients in this study to get the most out of their developmental experiences.

6. *Manage the entire coaching process to ensure consistency and quality.* Although it is important to let each coaching relationship unfold according to the individual needs of the clients, it is equally important to effectively manage the overall coaching process. Participation in coaching should be completely voluntary; however, once someone has committed to coaching, he or she should have specific expectations and guidelines for how the coaching will be conducted. Certain activities should be mandatory. The initial in-

person coaching introduction session should be made mandatory. Guidelines for conducting coaching should be established and followed. Each coaching session, for example, should be scheduled for a minimum of one hour. Sessions should be scheduled in advance, and clients should be prompt in calling at the appointed time. Client's line managers also have an important role in the developmental process and, at a minimum, should have one formal review session with their employee about coaching progress. Clients who reported doing this with their managers said that it increased mutual understanding of the outcomes and benefits of coaching.

7. *Build performance measurement into the coaching process.* The present study was conducted months after most of the coaching had been completed. Results of this study show that coaching is an effective and powerful developmental tool. Putting into place a performance measurement process at the beginning of coaching opens new learning opportunities for making coaching more effective while the coaching is being conducted. Coaching can be refocused to deal with issues or to ensure that business priorities will be met. Assessing the initial reactions of the clients to their coaching, for example, will provide insights into how best these clients may later apply what they have learned to their specific business issues. These insights will lead to actions that will ensure business-focused application of learning. Likewise, assessing how well the clients are applying what they have learned to their business will provide advanced notice on what the potential business impact may be. If the expected business outcomes seem unlikely to be realized, then midcourse corrections can be taken to make sure that company goals will be met.

CONCLUSION

Coaching was successful for the company. Certainly, the program more than paid for itself (788% ROI), with monetary benefits coming primarily from increases in work output, employee retention, and productivity. Although those clients who had customer or people responsibilities produced proportionally greater monetary benefits, the realization of these benefits to the business was fairly widespread throughout the group involved in this study. These business benefits from coaching can be traced back to the solid foundation that both coaches and clients created for themselves. Coaching sessions were rich learning environments that enabled the learning to be applied to a variety of business situations. Decision making, team performance, and the motivation of others were enhanced. Many of these business applications contributed annualized monetary benefits to the company. Other applications created significant intangible benefits. Overall, the clients appreciated their coaching experiences and would highly recommend coaching to others.

CHAPTER 12

Organization Capability: The ROI of Aligning an Organization to Strategy

INTRODUCTION

The new vice president of the inventory and distribution unit of a computer products manufacturer was sweating bullets. He had just come from a meeting with the CEO, who wanted to know why inventory had mushroomed to more than $300 million from $200 million in just one quarter. In part, the vice president knew the answer. His new leadership team had been scouring the nooks and crannies of the worldwide organization to hunt down and record every piece of inventory. These inventory items consisted primarily of parts for the many computer products that the company manufactured and distributed worldwide. The big increase of inventory valuation was really a good thing, the vice president thought, and showed just how diligent his team had been in documenting inventory. The CEO offered an alternative perspective that the vice president's organization seemed out of control.

True, inventory costs were high, turns were low, and the situation did not seem close to being turned around. The vice president, still new in his job, knew that his honeymoon period with the CEO was short-lived. Documenting the problem was not enough. Fixing the problem was the order of the day. But how? And what really was the problem? Poor inventory performance was likely the symptom of underlying and deeper problems.

The vice president summoned his leadership team to share and review all that they had learned during the inventory documentation process. They concluded that the traditional role of their organization—tracking and shipping parts on demand—was out of phase with the current needs of the business. Line business leaders were now looking for more comprehensive logistics solutions. FedEx can handle parts distribution. The leadership team decided to transform their organization from being a "parts is parts" supplier to becoming a logistics consultant. They changed the name of their unit to Global Logistics Services and developed a strategy to transform their organization. Over the course of several months, the leadership team took actions to implement the new strategy. Inventory levels topped $350 million. The CEO was getting impatient. One question loomed large: Are they capable as an organization of carrying out the strategy?

Diagnosis and Design: The Change Process Begins

The vice president picked up his telephone and called the vice president of organization development. Together, they worked out a plan to answer the capability question. A diagnosis was launched. The OD team conducted several interviews with a wide variety of people in the worldwide logistics organization and from their various internal customer groups. These interviews and other data collection efforts quickly got to the heart of the matter: Global Logistics was not capable of providing the logistics consulting the organization needed. Several issues were uncovered. People in the logistics organization were unclear about the new strategy and their new roles and responsibilities. Internal customers (such as field engineers) had been stockpiling inventory because they felt they weren't getting the logistics solutions they needed. Stockpiling inventory was costly, but customers had little faith that their need for timely access to parts would be met any other way. The diagnosis raised several key questions: What does the logistics organization need to be capable of doing, what are the most critical capability gaps, and how can these gaps be closed?

An organization capability assessment and alignment initiative was proposed to the leadership team. The business case cited numerous potential intangible benefits, including a strategically aligned organization, increased customer and employee satisfaction, and improved teamwork. The OD team committed to generate monetary benefits that would outweigh the investment made in the initiative. The initiative was approved for immediate action. This initiative consisted of two process steps: (1) develop a change plan that would close the most critical capability gaps, and (2) deploy the change plan, close the capability gaps, and better align the organization to the strategy. The OD team also agreed to evaluate the success of the initiative, determine the ROI, and prepare a final report to the logistics leadership team.

DEVELOPMENT: ALIGNING THE ORGANIZATION TO STRATEGY

It was clear that the Global Logistics organization was not capable of executing its new strategy, but what capabilities were required and how did Global Logistics stack up against these capabilities? Understanding where the logistics organization falls short will suggest actions to close the most strategically critical gaps. Developing a change plan to close the capability gaps was done in three steps:

1. Identifying a set of the required capabilities to achieve the strategy
2. Assessing the strategically most critical capabilities
3. Developing a change plan that states specifically what must be done to close the capability gaps

Identifying Organization Capabilities

The assessment phase began by the OD team first conducting a comprehensive assessment of what capabilities were required to provide logistics consulting. Interviews were conducted with people both inside and outside of the organization. Companies recognized as being world class in the logistics consulting and inventory management arenas were examined. Best practices were documented. This data collection resulted in a set of 20 capabilities. An example of a capability was: the ability to track trends in retail point-of-sale equipment faults. Twenty capabilities are too much for any leadership team to work on at once. Besides, the leadership team believed that they were better at some capabilities than others. A process to place these capabilities in priority order was needed. Then the leadership team could work on building those organization capabilities that would have the greatest strategic impact.

Assessing the Strategically Most Critical Capabilities

The leadership team was assembled with several other people from within and without Global Logistics. This extended team went through the process facilitated by the OD vice president that assessed each of 20 capabilities along two dimensions. The first dimension was how important the capability was to the specific strategy of the Global Logistics organization. The second dimension was how well they performed the capability as compared to their competitors. A two-dimensional grid was created to display these assessments (see Figure 12.1). Comparisons to competition ranged from deficient to superior, with parity representing middle ground. Criticality to strategy ranged from capabilities that were of lower strategic importance to those that were of higher strategic importance.

The assessment grid visually organized the 20 capabilities into three broad categories. Each dot in the figure represents a capability. The shaded area in the figure represents the first category of capabilities. The capabilities in the shaded area are those capabilities that are aligned to the strategy. That is, the more strategically important the capability, the better the organization is at performing this capability than its competitors. Conversely, capabilities of lesser strategic importance are not performed significantly better than their competitors perform these capabilities.

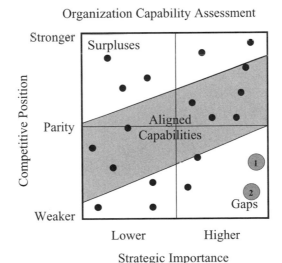

Figure 12.1 Assessment of 20 organization capabilities.

The second category of capabilities is represented by those capabilities that are considered to be surpluses in the organization. That is, these capabilities have minimum strategic importance, and yet these capabilities are performed at a higher level than the competition. It is acceptable—in fact, even desirable—to perform these capabilities at an industry average level. Why waste resources being really good at a capability when it does nothing for the business strategically? Moreover, resources could be redeployed from surplus capabilities to address capability gaps.

The third category of capabilities represents gaps in performance. These are capabilities that are strategically most important and yet are those being performed at a level below that of the competition. Returning to Figure 12.1, it can be seen that there are three, possibly four capabilities that fit this category, and of these four, two are especially troublesome. These two capabilities are enlarged in the figure and read:

1. The ability of logistics consultants to effectively satisfy the true needs of their customers with comprehensive logistics solutions
2. The ability to anticipate parts shortages for all product lines worldwide

These two capabilities were viewed as representing the old and the new of the Global Logistics organization. The first capability represented the new. Moving to becoming logistics consultants and offering a series of logistics services required a fundamental shift in how these consultants worked with their (mostly) internal customers. These consultants had, until recently, been purveyors of parts—taking the orders and scheduling delivery. These consultants had to quickly grasp how to meet their customers' needs with the new logistics services offerings.

The second capability represented the old. The leadership team recognized that they had to immediately stop the bleeding of inventory. Very few people would be willing to listen to the advice of logistics consultants offering new services when they are knee deep in inventory.

Developing the Change Plan

The leadership team examined both of these capabilities in more detail. Focus groups were convened to complete the picture of what each gap looked like and what it would take to close the gap. With regard to the first capability, logistics consultants were consultants in title only. As a group, they had little understanding of the consulting process or how to work with a client. The six new logistics solutions were also a big mystery to them. They did not feel comfortable talking with clients about these solutions and were not clear about the potential benefits of these solutions for their clients.

With regard to the second capability, the focus groups revealed that there were two main constraints to more efficient inventory management: data entry and exception reporting. Although the technical fix to these constraints was fairly straightforward, the tactical, or people, fix would be more challenging. Apparently, people had wrestled for years with the "garbage in, garbage out" problem with little success to show for their efforts. Many people had simply given up trying to order parts just in time, so instead they ordered parts by the ton and stored these parts in every nook and cranny of company property. One person in Paris, France rented a larger apartment so he could keep more parts. The situation was, as the CEO surmised, out of control.

An overall organization alignment plan was developed to close these capability gaps, but implementing this plan would require additional resources. This is where the surpluses came into play. The leadership team looked at the surplus capabilities and quickly found some low-hanging fruit of cost savings. These were capabilities that were being overinvested in with little tangible return to show for the investment. Ways were quickly found to recoup people's time and budget dollars. These resources were then redeployed to close the two top capability gaps.

The organization alignment plan detailed how specific actions regarding business processes, organization structure, people policies and practices, and reward mechanisms would be taken to build both capabilities. Table 12.1 summarizes the action plans for each of the capabilities. This table shows that building capabilities was viewed as a holistic enterprise and affected many aspects of the organization. Specific performance indicators were identified for each capability and tracking mechanisms put in place to provide monthly reporting on performance. The leadership team signed off on the design of the change plan and the indicators and agreed to move forward with the plan for transforming logistics services.

DEPLOYMENT: TRANSFORMATIONAL CHANGE AT GLOBAL LOGISTICS SERVICES

The first step that the change team took to implement the plan was to prepare the organization for the change. Communication messages were

Table 12.1 Organization Capability Alignment Plan

Capability Gaps	Process	Structure	People	Rewards
The ability of logistics consultants to effectively satisfy the true needs of their customers with comprehensive logistics solutions	Develop and deploy new consultative selling process, including new roles and responsibilities for logistics consultants.	Establish a new position of logistics solutions manager for each of six types of solution offerings.	Conduct workshops for all logistics consultants so they can perform the new consultative selling process and access information on solution offerings.	Reconfigure compensation to base 30% of annual bonus on deployment of new logistics services.
The ability to anticipate parts shortages for all product lines worldwide	Redesign parts tracking process to ease data entry operations and produce daily exception reports for field engineering managers.	Reemphasize responsibilities of field engineering managers to maintain data integrity; monitor daily potential parts shortages; and proactively place orders for new parts.	Conduct a series of conference calls with field engineering managers to implement the new responsibilities and work through any issues that they may raise.	Ensure that performance appraisals of the field engineering managers include performance on the three stated responsibilities. Consider increased bonus for those who reduce express air shipping charges.

developed and delivered through many different communication channels. The basic theme of these messages was simple: "If we do not change, we will be outsourced." Newsletters, town hall meetings, conference calls, videos, and the intranet were utilized to deliver the communication messages. Studies showed that people got the message and were prepared for action.

The next step was to organize two core change teams, one for each capability. People from many functional areas participated in these teams to successfully close a capability gap: human resources, accounting, information systems, and others. OD team members served as coaches to leadership team members to facilitate leading the change effort. The OD team also conducted a series of change management workshops for leaders and managers to build change agency as a competence. The results of all these efforts paid off. The change plan was implemented in about four months' time and by all accounts was viewed as successful.

REFLECTION: EVALUATING THE ROI OF STRATEGIC CHANGE

A formal evaluation was conducted on the financial benefits produced by the change efforts. Performance indicators for each capability were tracked, beginning with a base period before deployment and then reported each month during and after deployment. After six months had passed, all of the financial benefits were tallied. These financial benefits did not include over $1 million of one-time cost reductions that were made as a result of the change initiative. A focus group of leadership team members and other participants in the change process estimated the contribution that the change effort made to achieve these benefits. They estimated that 50% of the benefits resulted from the change initiative, and they were 100% confident in their estimate. The total program costs were tabulated and the ROI was calculated. The results were as follows:

Capability: The ability of logistics consultants to effectively satisfy the true needs of their customers with comprehensive logistics solutions
Qualified Benefits = $2.0 million × 50% contribution × 100% confidence = $1.0 million

Capability: The ability to anticipate parts shortages for all product lines worldwide
Qualified Benefits = $4.6 million × 50% contribution × 100% confidence = $2.3 million

Total qualified benefits = $3.3 million
Total initiative cost = $.3 million

$$ROI = (($3.3 \text{ million} - \$.3 \text{ million}) \div \$3 \text{ million}) \times 100 = 1000\%$$

The ROI of 1000% was a strong testament to the hard work and pioneering vision of the entire logistics services team. As impressive as this ROI was, the amount of qualified benefits, $3.3 million, paled in comparison to the benefits to be realized by bringing inventory under control. The $200 million inventory problem was worth about $20 million annually (given a 10% cost of money qualifier). At the close of the tracking period, these inventory levels appeared to be going down, but the time lag from the actions taken as a result of the initiative to having bottom-line impact on inventory levels pushed these benefits beyond the tracking period. So in terms of the initiative, the benefits associated with reductions in inventory levels were considered to be intangible. Other intangible benefits included improved leadership capability, increased competence in change management, more effective communication processes, clearer roles and responsibilities, and improved problem solving. Perhaps the biggest intangible benefit of all was left unsaid: The organization was not outsourced.

The logistics VP also earned high marks with the CEO. The CEO was still perturbed that inventory levels were too high, but he felt confident that the logistics VP had a firm handle on the problem and was making significant progress.

CHAPTER 13

Knowledge Management: The ROI of Continuously Leveraging Knowledge

INTRODUCTION

Knowledge is power, and knowledge management is a powerful, profitable business tool. A large equipment manufacturer realized an ROI of more than 400% by strategically leveraging knowledge throughout the corporation. Benefits were examined in two of the manufacturer's more than 200 communities of practice and these benefits are in the early stages of being accrued. The total value of this knowledge management program, then, is likely to be much greater in the near future.

This study of the knowledge management capability for the company examined in detail the bottom-line value of an Internet-based strategic business asset that captured and disseminated knowledge throughout the company. Intangible benefits were also revealed that included increased customer satisfaction with the company's equipment, strengthened dealer relationships, increased retention of people and knowledge, and continual learning.

DIAGNOSIS: UNDERSTANDING THE NEED FOR KNOWLEDGE MANAGEMENT

The company set continual learning as one of its key business objectives. Many distinct business units manufacture over-thirty large equipment products for customers around the world. The knowledge management network was created to enable company employees and its dealers to collaborate across lines of business and geographies. More frequent and timelier collaboration was expedited to improve the quality and execution of the design, engineering, building, and maintenance of the company's products.

The knowledge management network began as an information exchange tool for the company's engineers. It was transformed into a corporatewide strategic asset with innovative design features that reflect the manufacturer's business environment and contribute to the integration of knowledge management into the functioning of business processes and decision making.

Design of the Knowledge Management Network

The company took a fairly simple idea—exchanging knowledge among employees—and made it a standard business practice by formalizing the concept through the establishment of communities of practice, knowledge entries, and community discussions:

☐ *Communities of practice.* More than 200 communities of practice, organized around a specific business-related topic, were developed and have been accessed by more than 15,000 of the manufacturer's employees and dealers. A community manager oversees the development and maintenance of the community, controls access, and monitors content. Anybody with community access may initiate a threaded discussion involving members from around the world. Automatic e-mail updates of new material posted in the community are sent to community members.

Members access the community, read a threaded discussion and possibly make a contribution. The discussion thread grows as more members contribute. The thread completes when the original issue is resolved.

☐ *Knowledge entries.* People may post knowledge entries that pertain to a specific work process, tool, engineering problem or solution, quality issue, or other questions or problems. Entries are validated pieces of information that must be approved by the community manager. As the number of knowledge entries grows, so does the repository of knowledge.

☐ *Community discussion.* Bulletin boards enable outside experts, suppliers, partners, and others to post information relevant to the community. People may view these bulletin boards to gain access to required expertise.

The knowledge management network rapidly gained acceptance to become an integral part of how this manufacturer does business.

Development of Evaluation Objectives

Evaluation of the knowledge management was intended both to document the financial and intangible value that knowledge management created for the business and to make recommendations about how to accelerate this value creation. The ROI is based on annualized net benefits produced by people using knowledge management, factoring in the annual costs associated with supporting knowledge management.

DEPLOYMENT AND EVALUATION

Knowledge management enabled people to quickly engage the expertise and knowledge necessary to solve complex technical problems. By initiating a discussion thread, a member collaborates with other community members who contribute ideas and resources to the discussion thread. This ready collaboration, which has no geographic limitations, enables the discussion issue to be addressed more quickly and, in many cases, differently than would have happened without using the knowledge management.

Documenting financial benefits was accomplished on a case-by-case basis for two communities of practice. The joints and fasteners community was selected for study because it was a mature community, one of the five most active, and dealt with a core area of the manufacturing business. The second community selected was the dealer service community, which was chosen because it was one of the newer and less active communities and dealt with a support group.

The threaded discussions of each community were examined and selected for inclusion in the study if there was at least one response to the thread originator and the thread was not merely informational in nature (e.g., distributing meeting notes or giving notice of a meeting). The following list profiles the sampling of each community of practice. There were a total of 180 members in the joints and fasteners community, who generated 50 discussion threads. Twenty-four threads were selected for inclusion in the study. One person declined to participate in the study, resulting in 23 discussion threads being explored for this study (96% response rate). There were a total of 60 people in the dealer service community, who produced 15 dicussion threads. Five threads were selected for the study and 5 participated (100% response rate).

Joints and fasteners community

Total membership	180
Total discussion threads	50
Discussion threads selected	24
Threads included in study	23

Dealer service community

Total membership	60
Total discussion threads	15
Discussion threads selected	5
Threads included in study	5

Financial Benefits of Using the Knowledge Management

The study examined five areas of potential benefits: personal productivity, productivity of others, speed of problem resolution, cost savings, and quality. Each thread initiator was interviewed over the telephone to determine the financial benefit that was realized from resolving the threaded discussion issue. A descriptive chain of impact was drawn from utilizing knowledge management to producing annualized financial business benefits. Each thread initiator estimated the percentage of these benefits that were directly attributable to knowledge management. Then the thread initiator was asked to estimate (in a percentage) how confident he or she was in that estimate. The total financial benefit was multiplied by these two percentages. In this way the financial benefits were qualified, or discounted, to reflect only those benefits directly resulting from use of knowledge management. Thread initiators were also asked for third-party verification sources. Benefits verification was done for the larger financial benefits. Detailed examples of each of these five benefit areas will now be presented.

PERSONAL PRODUCTIVITY

Personal productivity was defined as the number of hours saved resolving the issue because of the knowledge management network—the difference between the time it took to resolve an issue using knowledge management compared to the time involved if knowledge management was not available and the thread initiator had to resolve the issue using other means. The most frequent answers were that the time to find the answer was reduced and that the quality of the answer was better than it would have been without knowledge management.

For example, one respondent said that he saved 24 hours of his time by using knowledge management because he did not have to send numerous e-mails and play phone tag with several of the contacts in his existing network. Moreover, he expanded his network of key resources by getting responses from two of the company's top metallurgists who had not earlier been in his informal network of contacts. The standard value for an hour of time was determined to be $65.

$$24 \text{ hours} \times \$65 \text{ per hour} = \$1560$$

The influence of knowledge management to produce this productivity gain was based on the respondent's estimations.

$$\$1560 \times 100\% \text{ contribution} \times 70\% \text{ confidence} = \$1092$$

The value of $1092 was added to the benefits tally.

PRODUCTIVITY OF OTHERS

This was defined as the number of hours of time that others saved as a result of the thread initiator resolving the issue using knowledge management. Without the knowledge management network, the person with the issue would have called others in his or her personal network in an effort to resolve the issue. Many of these calls would have produced negligible results, wasting time for both parties. Moreover, there is no guarantee that anyone in the personal network would have the information to address the issue. With the knowledge management capability, all community members receive a short question in their e-mail. Those who do not have anything to contribute simply ignore the message, whereas those who can contribute respond to the discussion thread.

One respondent said that by getting the answer so quickly using knowledge management, he saved at least a week of design time. This enabled designers to work on other design priorities.

$$40 \text{ hours} \times \$65 \text{ per hour} = \$2600$$

The influence of knowledge management to produce this productivity gain was based on the respondent's estimations.

$$\$2600 \times 100\% \text{ contribution} \times 75\% \text{ confidence} = \$1950$$

The value of $1950 was added to the benefits tally.

An important intangible benefit is how people share the solution of the issue with others. For example, one respondent noted: "After getting the answer, I shared it with others in my group who were not aware of this type of torque measuring."

SPEED OF PROBLEM RESOLUTION

This was defined as benefits produced as a result of accelerating the achievement of the solution by using knowledge management. In one example, a production supervisor rapidly gained needed expertise to resolve a problem. A new production line consisting of three workers had ground to a halt without a solution to this problem. Utilizing the knowledge management capability got the problem solved and the line back in production. The supervisor estimated the benefits to be at least $2000, attributed 100% to knowledge management and was 65% confident in the estimate.

$$\$2000 \times 100\% \text{ contribution} \times 65\% \text{ confidence} = \$1300$$

A benefit of $1300 was added to the benefits tally. An important intangible benefit was the production team being able to meet their new product introduction date. According to the supervisor, this likely would not have happened if he were unable to utilize knowledge management.

COST SAVINGS

This was defined as how the use of knowledge management contributed reducing costs. In one particularly well-documented example, a respondent utilized knowledge management to redesign a part for cylinders used in mining equipment. This person said, "If they had pursued the original design, the product would have failed in the field. This would have led to big rework costs."

Several people in the company's engineering and finance departments determined just how big the cost would have been. Blueprints of the part in question were obtained and experts consulted in determining the cost. The company produces 1000 units per year, and at least half of the units would have been reworked through a recall program. The cost of a similar part in another unit is $250, which does not include any labor or travel time for the repair.

$$1000 \text{ units} \div 50\% = 500 \text{ reworked units}$$

$$500 \text{ units} \times \$250 = \$125,000 \text{ unqualified benefits}$$

$$\$125,000 \times 100\% \text{ contribution} \times 50\% \text{ confidence} = \$62,500 \text{ qualified benefits}$$

The value of $62,500 was the highest extreme value and was therefore not included in total benefits tally.

QUALITY

The use of knowledge management to improve the quality of the product was documented. For example, a thread initiator was about to upgrade the specifications of a part. He first initiated a discussion on the knowledge management network and received a wealth of information that he would not have received without using knowledge management. He incorporated many of these ideas into the redesign, significantly improving the quality and customer acceptance of the part. These quality changes (resulting from use of knowledge management) were conservatively determined to be $4000. The thread initiator attributed 100% of this value to the knowledge management network and was 80% confident in that estimate.

$$\$4000 \times 100\% \times 80\% = \$3200$$

A total of $3200 was added to the benefits tally.

The qualified financial benefits were tallied for each of the five benefit categories. Table 13.1 presents these benefits for both communities. Combined, these communities produced $104,200 in benefits to the business.

Table 13.1 Qualified Financial Benefits of Both Communities of Practice

Community of Practice	Personal Productivity	Productivity of Others	Speed	Cost	Quality	Total
Joints and Fasteners	$22,000	$16,000	$8,000	$12,000	$3,200	$61,200
Dealer Service	$8,000	$10,000	$9,000	$16,000	0	$43,000
Total						$104,200

Annualized Costs of the Knowledge Management Network

In order to calculate the ROI, the annualized cost of managing and maintaining the two communities in this study must be determined. Given that these communities vary in size, pro rata cost must be used. Determining the annualized pro rata cost of utilizing knowledge management was done by dividing the total annual budget ($970,000) for knowledge management by the number of users (15,000) to yield $64.66. There were 180 members in the joints and fasteners community. Multiplying 180 times $65 = $11,700. There were 60 members in the dealer service training community. Multiplying 60 times $65 = $3900.

Calculating the Return on Investment

Return on investment and benefits/cost ratios were calculated for each community according to the following formulas:

$$ROI = ((\text{Benefits} - \text{Cost}) / \text{Cost}) \times 100$$

$$BCR = \text{Benefits} \div \text{Cost}$$

Joints and fasteners community

$$ROI = ((\$61,200 - \$11,700) \div \$11,700) \times 100 = 423\%$$

$$BCR = \$61,200 \div \$11,700 = 5.2 : 1$$

Dealer service community

$$ROI = (($43,000 - $3900) \div $3900) \times 100 = 1003\%$$
$$BCR = $43000 \div $3900 = 11:1$$

Estimating the Total Value of Knowledge Management

The client was also interested in the total annualized value that knowledge management contributed to the business. Estimating this value followed a three-step process. The first step was to calculate the average monetary benefit produced per the total number of threads initiated. The calculations for the two communities were as follows:
Joints and fasteners

$$$61,200 \div 50 \text{ Total Threads} = $1224$$

Dealer service

$$$43,000 \div 15 \text{ Total Threads} = $2867$$

The next step was to determine the total number of threads that were initiated for the previous 12 months. A 12-month figure was used here because we are dealing with annualized benefits. The system administrator tallied 3100 discussion threads that were initiated for the previous 12 months.

$$\text{Total Threads for 12-Month Period} = 3100$$

The third step was to calculate the total annualized value for knowledge management. This was accomplished by calculating the total value that each community contributes annually. These figures were treated as upper and lower estimates of the total value of knowledge management. The mean of the two was considered the best estimate of the total value that knowledge management makes to the business. The calculations were as follows:

Lower Limit of Estimate = $3100 \times $1224 = $3,794,400

Upper Limit of Estimate = $3100 \times $2867 = $8,887,700

Mean of Estimate   = $6,341,050

Calculating the ROI based on the mean of estimate figure was done as follows:

$$ROI = (($6,341,050 - $970,000) \div $970,000) \times 100 = 554\%$$

$$BCR = $6,341,050 \div $970,000 = 6.5:1$$

Intangible Benefits

Knowledge management made it possible for workers in distant and disparate facilities to share expertise. The knowledge management capability enabled collaboration among company employees in South America, Europe, Asia, and multiple facilities in the United States. Workers in facilities that did not have their own large engineering staffs were able to access information via the knowledge management capability. Without the network, these people would likely have to go outside the company for information. One younger engineer from a smaller facility said it was wonderful that in-house experts (citing two by name) were available to those engineers who are just getting started. This accelerated their learning curve and sped generational knowledge transfer. Other intangible benefits included:

- ☐ Improved collaboration skills and expansion of networking
- ☐ Improved customer satisfaction with the product
- ☐ Strengthened dealer relationships
- ☐ Strengthened foundation for value-chain integration
- ☐ Provided continual learning
- ☐ Improved retention of people
- ☐ Minimized loss of knowledge resulting from retirement of technical and engineering people

Reflection and Improvement Opportunities

Knowledge management produced significant value to the business. Benefits of the two communities in this study, drawn from more than 200 communities in the network, produced financial benefits ($104,200) that more than covered the cost of operating the network for these two communities ($15,600). Moreover, the preliminary analysis of the total value that knowledge management is creating for the business revealed an ROI of 554%. Throughout the course of this study, ways were identified for knowledge management to produce even greater benefits for the business:

- [ ] *Invest in developing community managers.* The formal review of the two communities in this study and the informal review of several other communities underscored the critical role that community managers played in growing a robust community. Managers who were active, highly engaged in leveraging knowledge, and served as role models for community participation were those who grew robust communities. Being a community manager means more than just providing administrative support; it means taking an active, passionate role in building a strategic capability for the business. The two communities in this study were fortunate to have two such managers at their helm. The practice of knowledge management would benefit from determining the characteristics of highly effective community managers and providing developmental opportunities for all active community managers so they can become even more effective. This study clearly shows that any such investment would produce a significant financial return, most likely paying for the development effort many times over.

- [ ] *Celebrate successes and highlight accomplishments.* The communities of practice likely generate important successes every month. Those who use knowledge management experience success, and this positive experience encourages their use of the network in the future. Providing more public recognition for these successes will further reinforce community participation and increase community membership.

- [ ] *Seed some communities based on business need.* It is important to ask the question if all of the communities are in place to accomplish the company's strategy. All communities can be reviewed and mapped to the strategy. If there are gaps in community support for the strategy, new communities should be started to close the gaps. Although it is great that communities have self-generated according to perceived needs by the employees, this approach can be supplemented by a more proactive approach by business leaders to maximize the business value of knowledge management.

- [ ] *Provide a select group of strategic communities with added support.* Criteria can be established to rank the strategic importance of the communities. Consideration can be given to provide administrative support to those communities of the greatest strategic importance. This kind of support would free up community managers from their transactional and administrative duties so they could focus more of their efforts on leveraging the strategic value of their communities.

☐ *Set standards for operation and cull inactive communities.* More than 200 communities of practice have been initiated, but the informal review of many of these communities indicated that many are inactive. Standards for maintaining a community can be developed, and communities can be evaluated against these standards regularly. This evaluation could result in deactivating (non-strategic) communities, which would provide added focus and resources on the active communities. Actively refreshing communities ensures that the entire knowledge management capability is a robust and efficient creator of value for the business.

CHAPTER 14

How Leaders and Change Practitioners Work Together to Create Strategic Value

EARNING A SEAT AT THE TABLE

Most strategic change practitioners do not have a seat waiting for them at senior leadership conference tables. This is unfortunate because there has never been a time when implementing strategic change has been so important—even essential—for business success. Virtually every strategic business decision has a human capital component. Making business decisions without fully considering and leveraging human capital surely suboptimizes these decisions and their implementation. Sources of competitive advantage remain untapped. Change practitioners have the knowledge and tools in their arsenal to make strategically critical contributions to better leverage human capital and seize competitive advantage.

What will it take for strategic change practitioners to get a seat at the table? First of all, the invitation for the seat must be earned. At the senior leadership level, with the stakes set so high, there are no free passes. Change practitioners must prove themselves to be indispensable partners in achieving extraordinary business results. Earning a seat at the leadership table requires change practitioners to get heard, gain credibility, and deliver results. Table 14.1 highlights the nine essential practices of successful change practitioners organized by these three areas.

Table 14.1 Nine Essential Practices of Successful Change Practitioners

Getting Heard	Gaining Credibility	Delivering Results
1. Give them the numbers.	4. Show you care.	7. Recognize that perceptions are reality.
2. Tell stories.	5. Develop a point of view.	8. Manage risk factors.
3. Don't forget the punchline.	6. Avoid going native.	9. Connect the dots.

Getting Heard

GIVE THEM THE NUMBERS

Business leaders routinely base investment decisions on ROI calculations or estimates. Yet, this measurement discipline has often not been applied to decisions regarding strategic change. Why? In part, change practitioners have been reluctant to embrace evaluation as an important aspect of the change process. Many change practitioners have not been trained in the language of numbers and may even be intimidated to express their work in numbers. They lament that too much of the true value they create is lost in the translation to numbers. To some extent this is true. Like with any language translation, some meaning will be lost. This does not diminish OD work; it just offers another language for talking about the value that OD provides. Plus, this language has meaning for business leaders. Gaining credibility with these leaders requires that change practitioners talk their language.

ROI is an important aspect of the conversation that change practitioners have with business leaders. Numbers are often foremost for business leaders and a starting point to engage in a broader conversation about the strategic value of a change initiative. Numbers are not reality; in fact, numbers are an abstraction of reality. We use numbers to convey observations, develop insights, and share important information with each other. Some may suggest that because numbers cannot capture all that is truly important about strategic change, they should not enter the conversation. This suggestion misses the point. ROI is *one* aspect of the strategic change conversation; it is not the entire conversation. The ROI provides one part, and a very important part, of the overall picture of strategic change.

Tell Stories

Numbers are necessary but not sufficient for leaders to understand the scope, breadth, and implications of strategic change. Numbers bring the leaders to the water trough, but the compelling story makes them drink. During the course of the ROI analysis, several stories will emerge: a manager using the new sales process will land a major new customer account; an engineer joins a virtual community of practice and soon accesses the knowledge necessary to solve a longstanding and perplexing problem; and an emerging leader gains an insight from a coaching session that leads to a profitable new business opportunity. These great stories will resonate with business leaders. Stories convey the personal and emotional connection that people make with one another as they leverage the initiative in their work. Leaders see the connection from the initiative to the business on a human scale. The value from the initiative becomes real and heartfelt.

Don't Forget the Punchline

Presenting ROI information and compelling stories completes the quantitative and qualitative picture of how an initiative added value. Don't stop here and leave people guessing about the true meaning of your analysis. In a leadership team setting, focus people's attention on the key messages that you think should be taken from the information. Present information in a way that reinforces these key messages. Draw conclusions from the information and clearly state the implications of these conclusions to business leaders. Advocate your point of view and show how this is supported by the data. Describe in concrete terms what next steps should be taken. This is a time to shine. Leadership team members will appreciate your business savvy and challenging them to take actions to improve the business.

Gaining Credibility

Show You Care

People will often not listen to you until they know you care. One of the first ways of showing that you care is to become a student of the business. Demonstrate your interest in the business. Review the financials, read investment analysts' reports about the company, and investigate the competition and market trends. Show genuine interest in the company and its people. Draw implications from what you learn to how business leaders may be affected. If, for example, you learn that the price point for the company's main product is expected to drop by 25% in the next year, what are the implications for product development? When will new higher-margin products be available? Can a suite of services be wrapped around this main product to stem margin erosion? As a change practitioner, you are not expected to walk in right away with ready-made answers. The point here is that by doing your homework and asking the right questions, you are demonstrating that you care about the company and the leaders' ability to be successful.

DEVELOP A POINT OF VIEW

As you learn more about the company and ask important questions about the business, you may find certain courses of action more appealing than other courses of action. There is a point when inquiry gives way to advocacy. You think that you know enough to know what to do. Develop a point of view and be willing to advocate it. If, for example, it takes two years to develop a new product, it is unlikely that new products will be brought in early enough to boost margins for a rapidly fading product line. Advocate a fast-cycle product development initiative to bring in new products in six months. Don't just be a business tourist, making observations as you go. Be a forceful advocate for change. Make change happen.

AVOID GOING NATIVE

Change practitioners are most effective when they strike a balance between empathy and understanding for a business and its people on one hand, and objectivity and an external perspective on the other hand. This is a delicate balance. Remaining too objective may be seen as being aloof or even arrogant. People may listen to your message but harbor skepticism about your motives or whether you really care about them. Erring on the side of too much empathy may make you seem to be identifying with the problem rather than challenging people to find a solution. It is personally rewarding to be accepted by a group of people in an organization, but being an integral part of the group may diminish your ability to challenge the group to change. Trying too hard to fit into the group, or going native, runs the risk of losing the objectivity required to be an effective change agent and having the perceived independence to forcefully advocate for change.

Delivering Results

RECOGNIZE THAT PERCEPTIONS ARE REALITY

Each of us would like to think that we have a firm grasp on reality. We often tend to assume that our reality is shared by everyone else, but reality is a matter of perceptions, and we all perceive the world differently. The varying perceptions that people have about the organization, its issues, and each other are the realities with which all change practitioners must deal. Try to see the world from the perspectives of others. Avoid being judgmental. We tend to judge others by what they do, but we judge ourselves by our intentions. Flip this around. Enter into dialogues with others to learn about their intentions. Act as if they are well intentioned. Understand and appreciate their aspirations for the future. Then take a look at your own behavior. Suspend the safety net of your intentions. What did you do and not do; what effect did you have on others; how did your actions likely make others feel? Come to know how people are perceiving you through your actions. Explore what you must do differently to create different perceptions. This exercise will help you more effectively manage how others perceive you and the value that you provide the organization.

MANAGE RISK FACTORS

Investing in and deploying strategic change often represents a big risk for business leaders. There is the risk of squandering the investment, misdirecting resources, losing time to get products or services to market, and fear of losing competitive edge. Bottom-line OD opens up a new avenue for better managing the risk of strategic change. Building evaluation into the process of change management ensures that change objectives impact business objectives, ensures that the initiative is designed to achieve these objectives, and enables timely midcourse corrections to be made during deployment. Be sure to make these points with the business leaders. Position yourself and the evaluation component of the initiative as a way to better manage the financial risk of the investment in the initiative. During deployment, utilize the evaluation signposts as triggers to take corrective actions and effectively manage the risk of the investment.

CONNECT THE DOTS

Strategic change is complex. There are many data points to consider and to construct into a whole picture of strategic change. There are performance gaps, initiative objectives, evaluation objectives, pilot data, isolation factors, cost data, ROI analysis, and intangible benefits, just to name a few. All of these data points must align to the business goals. You, as a change practitioner, are in the unique position of being able to connect all of these data points, paint the whole picture, and determine the impact on the business goals. The final report issued by the change practitioner pulls the whole story together in a way that educates business leaders about the initiative and the business. This report has tremendous value, not only in the near term to leverage the value of the change initiative, but also in the long term to sustain and expand the value of strategic change. Take the lead in challenging business leaders to drive this value to the bottom line.

VALUES OF BOTTOM-LINE OD

The foundation for bottom-line OD and enacting these nine essential practices is based on three sets of values:

1. *People must value accountability for results.* Bottom-line OD increases and focuses this accountability to achieve organization goals.
2. *People must value feedback to drive even greater performance.* Bottom-line OD provides real-time feedback on the progress of change. Acting on this feedback to make midcourse corrections will increase the value of the initiative to the organization.
3. *People must value knowledge creation and learning.* Bottom-line OD generates a wealth of knowledge that in the short term leads to improving the initiative and in the long term leads to improving organization performance.

What Leaders Must Do to Live Bottom-Line OD Values

In 1994, a large natural resources company put pictures of several of its employees on the cover of its annual report and proclaimed: People are our greatest asset! Within months, plans to lay off more than 12,000 employees were announced. This "ain't walkin' the talk." In fact, the contrast between the talk and the walk was so stark that the leadership lost a lot of credibility in the eyes of the employees. As a result, the leaders' plans to organize support people (e.g., human resources, finance) into a fee-for-service concept was viewed by employees with great suspicion about the true motives of the leaders. Proclamations about restructuring for the future were met with great skepticism. People were not fully engaged in the change efforts and, in fact, felt disenfranchised in the process. Restructuring did not achieve its stated goals and the company was acquired five years later.

Leaders must walk the talk. It is not enough just to say how important people are to achieving company goals. Sincere action must follow. Leaders must stay the course with the people and change initiatives they launch. They cannot withdraw support for change initiatives at the first whiff of a company profit shortfall. Inconsistency dooms any investment, and change initiatives are no different. View change initiatives not just as a cost to be endured, but also as financial benefit to be realized.

When business conditions do become challenging, don't fold your tent and retreat. Respond by challenging those responsible for the change initiative to deliver more. If you as a leader want to maximize the value from people and change initiatives, recognize that the way you invest in these initiatives plays by the same rules as with hard-asset investments. Forecast a return on investment, make people accountable for achieving the financial return, bank on the expected outcome, and stay the course.

What Change Practitioners Must Do to Live Bottom-Line OD Values

As a change professional, accept as your responsibility to be an unrelenting advocate for sustainable strategic change. Recognize that you must earn the right every day to challenge the leaders and the organization to set bold goals and launch strategic change initiatives to achieve these goals. Be willing to accept the consequences. Welcome being held accountable for achieving numbers. All other businesspeople who sit at the leadership table do this. Bottom-line OD does not make you different from the others; in fact, it puts you on the same playing field with others, playing by the same rules.

Bottom-line OD provides a way for change practitioners to demonstrate the business impact of change initiatives. Change is not undertaken for its own sake, but rather to produce tangible business value. Change practitioners have a responsibility to openly accept feedback on what is not working well and, working with the business leaders, make the appropriate adjustments to the change process. This is not a time for defensiveness. It is a time to earn some stripes and show the leaders how much you value the stewardship of their assets and the delivery of the expected results. People earn a seat at the leadership table by taking accountability for results, rolling with the punches, and delivering the goods.

Accountability, Trust, Commitment, and Bottom-Line OD

Accountability can be both elusive and risky, and it is difficult for any single person—including the CEO—to accomplish valuable change without trust and cooperation. If people within an organization are going to take on the risk of accountability, they must believe that they can rely on and trust their team members. Consider the analogy of the "no-look" pass in basketball. A team member can throw the ball with confidence that a fellow player will be in place to catch the ball. He doesn't waste game time trying to locate support—he knows from experience that the team member will be in place—and he is willing to take the risk of this blind pass because all team members have accepted responsibility for the outcome. A basketball player wouldn't take the risk of throwing the ball if he anticipated its interception by the other team—if he believed he was alone in taking the risk. Similarly, team members in a business organization will take the risk of accountability when the risk is shared among trusted team members.

Accountability, then, must be shared. People must feel that others have "skin in the game"; they must *know* this. Sharing cannot be tacitly assumed; there must be an overt act of commitment and trust that establishes this shared accountability.

This is where bottom-line OD comes into play. In the evaluation process, expectations are expressed in tangible, measurable outcomes. Team members know where they need to be in order to correctly perform a no-look pass; they know what works and what doesn't. They know what their responsibilities are in the change process and how their performance will be measured collectively. They know what value will be created or affected by the actions they take. No one is wildly throwing balls in the hope that someone, somewhere will catch them. People are more likely to commit to change when they trust their partners in change. The evaluation process fosters increased levels of trust because it better defines success outcomes for individuals and makes explicit the expectations of leaders. People will better understand how their performance will be evaluated and what to expect from others. Expectations, evaluations, and the criteria for recognition are above board.

The evaluation process gives the change initiative traction. The concept, or reality, of change *du jour* is removed. Everyone achieves a sense of permanence—a sense that the change will stick—and will work harder to ensure that adhesion. No one wants to take the risk of change if it seems without merit or point. The evaluation process establishes the worth and meaning of the strategic change initiative and encourages continued efforts toward achieving the goal and realizing its potential. The "what's the point?" cynicism of proposed change is replaced with active, loyal participation. Evaluation that is an integral part of the organization's routine fosters a culture of accountability that leads to better and longer-sustained results.

Feedback, Performance, and Bottom-Line OD

Evaluation provides feedback on progress toward goals and consequently drives higher performance. It is difficult for people to maintain momentum and motivation to achieve goals if they do not know the effectiveness of their efforts or where their team stands. Imagine going to a basketball game where the ongoing score is never posted. Only when the final whistle is blown do the players know for sure who won and how their performance contributed to the outcome. When performance achievement is not measured and expectations remain uncertain, even highly motivated people are challenged to move forward productively.

Setting a measurable objective is one thing, but achieving it is another. The key to achieving an objective is receiving periodic and frequent feedback on your progress—checking the score of the basketball game as well as points, rebounds, and assists—so that any necessary midcourse corrections can be made. If at halftime, assists are very low, more must be done immediately to open up passing lanes and increase ball movement. Making these midcourse corrections not only enhances the likelihood of meeting the objective of winning the game, but it also makes the work more enjoyable, rewarding, and productive. Periodically evaluating each person's progress against the team goal helps build trust and reaffirms the commitment of each person to win the game and share accountability for the successful outcome.

Knowledge, Learning, and Bottom-Line OD

The evaluation process enables organization leaders to increase their learning quotient about how the company is performing; they gain frequent, important updates about who and what is working well and can act and react accordingly. Each evaluation process produces numbers that an organization leader can use—a stark reality check that tells a leader whether a change initiative is working or not as expected while there is still time to make changes. Conversely, the evaluation process can also have a steadying influence on an impatient leader who might too hastily abandon an initiative because its results and potential results aren't apparent. Sometimes a leader doesn't see results simply because the results have not been properly measured and presented. Feedback on performance helps the leader realize both the effectiveness of a current initiative as well as learn a great deal about the organization as a whole.

When the progress of a business strategy is made clear though an evaluation process, the potential for successful new strategies increases. The evaluation process increases the learning curve for all members of an organization; members have clear expectations, for which they are accountable, and leaders have solid insight about the organization's status and potential that neither could have without a reliable, routine evaluation procedure.

Bottom-line OD provides leaders and team members with the knowledge they need to effectively make strategic change happen. Participants in a given change initiative understand the connection between their actions and the overall organizational goals. The smoke clears, and the context for change becomes clearer. When an initiative is announced, it is no longer seen as a stand-alone proposition. Leaders don't have to struggle to motivate people by continually explaining the *whys* of an initiative. Throughout the evaluation process, participants know the reasons for an initiative and how they connect with it. The "why are we doing this?" lament can be more expediently replaced by the question: "How can we accomplish this?" When people have a shared understanding, they are more likely to develop a shared sense of commitment.

When leaders understand the interconnectedness of business goals and change initiatives, they can better focus the initiatives on achieving overall company goals. They can better utilize resources and, in the process, become more effective leaders. They aren't leading team members in what may appear to be many scattered directions or diluting people's energy by launching too many initiatives. Leaders see the big picture and launch initiatives to achieve business strategy.

None of this big picture thinking happens easily or by accident. In order for the evaluation process to be effective, it must be an integral part of the change initiative from the inception of the change. This is another way in which bottom-line OD makes a contribution. Building the discipline of evaluation into strategic change initiatives cannot be an afterthought but must begin as soon as the need for change is perceived. A change should not be implemented until a system for measuring the effectiveness of that change is in place. Evaluation shapes the initiative, not the other way around. The evaluation process creates a line of sight that is drawn from the business strategy to the change initiative objectives. The initiative is based on addressing read business needs. Evaluating the initiative is hardwired into achieving business strategy. Otherwise, change can veer off into any direction, and the initiative will short-circuit before the desired business strategy is achieved. Bottom-line OD prevents this kind of off-course meandering by drawing the best from evaluation methodology and integrating it with the design and deployment of complex strategic change.

Further Reading

Anderson, M.C. "The ROI of Knowledge Management," *ASTD Links*, 2002;1(5).

Anderson, M.C. *Strategic Change: Fast Cycle Organization Development* (Cincinnati, OH: South-Western, 2000).

Anderson, M.C. "Transforming Support Work into Competitive Advantage," *National Productivity Review*, Spring 1998;11–18.

Anderson, M.C., Dauss, C., and Mitsch, B. "The Return on Investment in Executive Coaching at Nortel Networks." In *In Action: Executive Coaching* (Alexandria, VA: American Society for Training and Development, 2002).

Anderson, M.C., Goelz, R., and Morrow, M. "Building Capability for Business Impact," *Organization Development Journal*, 1998;16(4):13–20.

Anderson, M.C., and Morrow, M. "Organization Capability: Creating Simplicity and Focus in Business Life," *Organization Development Journal*, 1997;15(1):72–81.

Argyris, C. *Knowledge for Action* (San Francisco: Jossey-Bass, 1993).

Argyris, C. *Overcoming Organizational Defenses* (Boston: Allyn and Bacon, 1990).

Argyris, C. *Reasoning, Learning and Action: Individual and Organizational* (San Fransisco: Jossey-Bass, 1982).

Argyris, C. "Double Loop Learning in Organizations," *Harvard Business Review*, 1977;65:115–125.

Beckhard, R., and Pritchard, W. *Changing the Essence* (San Francisco: Jossey-Bass, 1992).

Block, P. *Stewardship: Choosing Service over Self Interest* (San Francisco: Berrett-Koehler, 1993).

Block, P. *Flawless Consulting* (San Diego: Pfeiffer and Sons, 1981).

Brown, S.L., and Eisenhardt, K.M. *Competing on the Edge: Strategy as Structured Chaos* (Boston: Harvard Business School Press, 1998).

Campbell, D.T., and Stanley, J.C. *Experimental and Quasi-Experimental Designs for Research* (Chicago: Rand McNally, 1963).

Cummings, T.G., and Worley, C.G. *Organization Development and Change* (Cincinnati: South-Western, 2000).

Galbraith, J. *Designing Complex Organizations* (Reading, MA: Addison-Wesley, 1973).

Goldberg, B., and Sifonis, J.G. *Dynamic Planning: The Art of Managing Beyond Tomorrow* (New York: Oxford University Press, 1994).

Hassett, J. "Simplifying ROI," *Training*, 1992;September:54.

Hodges, T.K. *Linking Learning and Performance* (Boston: Butterworth–Heinemann, 2002).

Isaacs, W. *Dialogue and the Art of Thinking Together* (New York: Doubleday, 1999).

Kanter, R.M. *The Change Masters* (New York: Simon and Schuster, 1983).

Kirkpatrick, D.L. *Evaluating Training Programs* (San Francisco: Berrett-Koehler, 1998).

Kotter, J.P. *Leading Change* (Cambridge: Harvard Business School Press, 1996).

LaMarsh, J. *Changing the Way We Change: Gaining Control of Major Operational Change* (Reading, MA: Addison-Wesley, 1995).

Lynch, R.L., and Cross, K.F. *Measure Up! Yardsticks for Continuous Improvement* (Cambridge: Blackwell, 1991).

MacDonald, L. *Nortel Networks: How Innovation and Vision Created a Network Giant* (Etobicoke, Ontario: John Wiley & Sons, 2000).

Maister, D.M. *Professional Service Firm Management* (Boston: Maister Associates, 1990).

Meyer, C. *Relentless Growth* (New York: The Free Press, 1998).

Mitroff, I.I., Mason, R.O., and Pearson, C.M. *Framebreak: The Radical Redesign of American Business* (San Francisco: Jossey-Bass, 1994).

Mitsch, D.J. *In Action: Coaching for Extraordinary Results.* (Alexandria, VA: ASTD, 2002).

Nadler, D.A., and Tushman, M.L. *Strategic Organization Design* (New York: HarperCollins, 1988).

Nadler, L., and Wiggs, G.D. *Managing Human Resource Development* (San Francisco: Jossey-Bass, 1986).

Phillips, J.J. *Handbook of Training Evaluation and Measurement Methods*, 3rd ed. (Houston: Gulf Publishing, 1997).

Phillips, J.J. *Accountability in Human Resources Management* (Houston: Gulf Publishing, 1996).

Phillips, J.J. "Measuring ROI in an Established Program," *In Action: Measuring Return on Investment*, 1994;1:187–197.

Phillips, J.J., Stone, R.D., and Phillips, P.P. *The Human Resources Scorecard: Measuring the Return on Investment* (Boston: Butterworth–Heinemann, 2001).

Phillips, P.P. *The Bottomline on ROI* (Atlanta: CEP Press, 2002).

Porter, M.E. *Competitive Strategy: Techniques for Analyzing Industries and Competitors* (New York: Free Press, 1980).

Prahalad, C.K., and Hamel, G. "The Core Competence of the Corporation," *Harvard Business Review*, 1990;May/June:79–91.

Senge, P.M. *The Fifth Discipline: The Art and Science of the Learning Organization* (New York: Doubleday, 1990).

Stacey, R.D. *Managing the Unknowable* (San Francisco: Jossey-Bass, 1992).

Watkins, K.E., and Marsick, V.J. *Sculpting the Learning Organization* (San Francisco: Jossey-Bass, 1993).

List of Figures
and Tables

Index

223

About the Author

Dr. Merrill C. Anderson is a business consulting executive, author and educator with twenty years experience improving the performance of people and organizations. Dr. Anderson is currently the chief executive officer of MetrixGlobal LLC, a professional services firm that partners with business leaders to maximize the value of people and change initiatives. He specializes in providing business support groups such as human resources, corporate universities and training functions, organization development and quality with performance measurement solutions that increase accountability for bottom-line results. He has held senior executive positions with four *Fortune 500* firms including senior vice president of human resources, founding dean for a corporate university and vice president of organization development. Dr. Anderson has consulted with over one hundred companies throughout North America and Europe to effectively manage strategic organization change. He has over forty professional publications and speeches to his credit including the books *Strategic Change: Fast Cycle Organization Development* (South-Western College Publishing) and *In Action: Building Learning Capability Through Outsourcing* (ASTD). His new book *Bottom-Line Organization Development* breaks new ground in applying powerful evaluation methodology to increase bottom-line value from strategic change initiatives. Dr. Anderson is an elected member of the ASTD ROI Advisory Council and is clinical professor in education at

Drake University. He earned his doctorate at New York University, his masters degree at the University of Toronto and bachelors degree at the University of Colorado. He and his wife Dianna live in Johnston, Iowa with their two sons.

The Value of Belonging

ASTD membership keeps you up to date on the latest developments in your field, and provides top-quality, *practical* information to help you stay ahead of trends, polish your skills, measure your progress, demonstrate your effectiveness, and advance your career.

We give you what you need most from the entire scope of workplace learning and performance:

Information
We're your best resource for research, best practices, and background support materials – the data you need for your projects to excel.

Networking
We're the facilitator who puts you in touch with colleagues,experts, field specialists, and industry leaders – the people you need to know to succeed.

Technology
We're the clearinghouse for new technologies in training, learning, and knowledge management in the workplace – the background you need to stay ahead.

Analysis
We look at cutting-edge practices and programs and give you a balanced view of the latest tools and techniques – the understanding you need on what works and what doesn't.

Competitive Edge
ASTD is your leading resource on the issues and topics that are important to you. That's the value of belonging!

For more information, or to become a member, please call 1.800.628.2783 (U.S.) or +1.703.683.8100; visit our Website at www.astd.org; or send an email to customercare@astd.org.

Linking People,
Learning & Performance

000-31410